I0503587

SOCIAL MEDIA MARKETING FOR BUSINESS 2019

SOCIAL MEDIA MARKETING FOR BUSINESS 2019: NEW STRATEGIES TO MAKE MONEY ONLINE AND SHAPE THE FUTURE OF YOUR SMALL OR LARGE BUSINESS CAPITALIZING ON NEW FACEBOOK AND INSTAGRAM TRENDS.

Table of Contents

Description

Are you a business owner?

The heartbeat and pulse of every business endeavor are profits generated from increased SALES! Regardless of the nature, structure, and position of your business, one of the first things you will like to consider is finding the easiest, cheapest and fastest way to grow and steadily expand the network of your influence and customer base. The truth is, there are many marketing, income generation, and business promotion options out there, but all these have been taken over by significant technological breakthroughs of the 21st century. It is called Social Media Marketing and other Internet-based business platforms.

Do you want to drive traffic and increase sales?

Do you want to record reasonable sales in your business as much as establish your brand as the industry leader? Are you a personality that requires building a personal image online? Do you want to get the people conversing about you? Congratulations! You've found the right book: as the urge to help guide and train newbies and existing users on how to dive into this technological development inspired this.

There is a need to leverage on Internet, and social media platforms for business, passive income, marketing and promotion of your brand as social media can help you in dynamic ways beyond the capacity of traditional means of business promotion.

This book will primarily help expand your knowledge base on how businesses that care about their awareness and aim to get people conversing about them can do it as this is the first gap social media helps bridge. It brings your brand an opportunity to 'shoot your shot' at clients and thereby creating a reputation that will make you stay on the lips of users of social media and most importantly, your clients.

This guide will focus on the following:

- Preliminary Considerations
- Finding the Right Social Media Platform for Your Business
- Integrating Social Media into Your Omnichannel Marketing Strategy
- The Sales Conversion Process
- Facebook Marketing
- Instagram
- Twitter Marketing
- YouTube Marketing
- Flickr
- Tumblr
- Goodreads
- The Best Way to Approach Social Media Marketing... AND MORE!!!

Introduction

The purpose of social media for general users is fairly straightforward: you get on your chosen platform and begin to network with your friends and family. If you are looking to grow your network, you can add other people who are interested in similar things as you are and then become "digital friends" with them. In other words, you never actually meet them in person, but you share with them online on a consistent basis and get to know them through status updates, comments, and other social media conversations. It truly is about networking and, more importantly, *talking and sharing* with one another.

This is exactly what makes social media such a powerful platform for businesses to market their products on.

It has long been known that word of mouth is one of the most powerful marketing strategies at the disposal of any company. If you want to grow your business, having people share positive comments and experiences about your business while recommending you to others is a great way to start. Meanwhile, if they are sharing negative comments or bad experiences, that is a great way to end up running out of clients because people stop trusting you and, therefore, stop doing business with you. If you want to have success, then, you need to earn the positive comments and recommendations from people who have fallen in love with your business.

Since social media is already all about talking, sharing, and networking with others, it makes sense that this is an incredibly powerful platform to get on when it comes to marketing your business. People are already leveraging word of mouth; all you need to do is get on there and give them something to talk about. By creating a profile for your business and sharing content on a regular basis, you give people plenty to talk about through your profile. This way, all they need to do is engage with your business and share with others so that you are being seen by those who are most likely to purchase from you.

Because of the power of social media and the power of word of mouth, an incredible modern business has evolved from this system. That is: influencers. Becoming an influencer means taking on a business model where you are at the center of conversations, and you are the one influencing what people are talking about. Essentially, becoming an influencer means that you build your popularity on social media and then begin talking about products or services that you love, thus causing those who follow you to talk about them, too. Because you are popular and they already trust you, they are more likely to purchase these products or services.

Becoming an influencer gives you the opportunity to charge businesses for your endorsement, essentially meaning that you are paid a commission every time someone purchases something because you influenced them to. As a result, you can earn money solely through becoming popular on social media and then guiding people to purchase certain products or services through companies that are willing to pay you.

Both starting your own business giving something people to talk about or running a business where you influence people to talk about certain things, are great ways to get involved in social media marketing so that you can make a profit online. In this book, we are going to talk about how you can conquer both of these models online, allowing you to build the online business empire of your dreams, no matter what that might look like.

Choosing the Right Niche on Social Media

The first thing that you need to do when you begin to leverage social media for growing a business is find out what your niche is. A niche outlines a specific segment of your chosen industry that you are going to talk to, which is necessary if you are going to make an impact in social media marketing. Because billions of people use social media every month, and most industries are marketing to multiple millions of people, you need to have a specific segment of the market that you are talking to if you are going to be heard. Otherwise, people are going to ignore you because your information and updates do not feel personable enough for them to really relate with, connect to, and pay attention to you.

Choosing the right niche on social media is necessary regardless of where you are at in business or what business model you are using to make money online. However, there will be certain steps that you need to adjust if you are going to be developing a business online to ensure that you are choosing the niche that is going to give you the most opportunity to grow online.

If you already have a business that you have been running off of social media, choosing the right niche on social media is about finding the part of your audience that is most likely to pay attention to you in the online space. So, if your market is generally 30-40 year old women in person, you need to find out which types of women you are marketing to the most and who is spending the most time online, and then you need to focus your marketing efforts on them.

With a business already up and running, targeting your niche online is going to be incredibly simple because you already have statistics available to show you who pays the most attention to your marketing, and to your business in general. All you need to do is refine these statistics to identify who is online and what they are talking about so that you can find the right angle to talk with them online.

For example, Horace and Jasper is a leather company located in Calgary, Alberta. Their company creates belts, purses, bags, wallets, cellphone charms, wrist cuffs, and more. In reality, this company could market to just about anyone who would wear a belt or carry a wallet because of how versatile their products are. However, if they were to market to just anyone, they would not have any success in getting discovered online. Instead, they have decided to market specifically to edgy, punk rock type that is looking to shop local for products that are higher quality and backed with a more trustworthy guarantee. This way, they are speaking to a very specific segment of their possible market, which results in a massive amount of success in their marketing strategies and business growth.

Another great example of how this works is with the Honest Company. This company provides baby care and cleaning products that are cleaner, more environmentally friendly, and less harmful to your family. Ideally, they could market to anyone who lives in a house or who has young children because they are providing products that are relevant to these two segments of the market. However, they know that the people most likely to purchase their products are women who are environmentally conscious and who want to do better for their families. So, they tend to market toward women and moms who are wanting a safer alternative to harsh chemicals, which results in them having massive growth on their online platform, as well as their business in general.

Identifying your niche is less about paring down and finding one single type of person to talk to, and more about identifying the angle that you use on social media. You want to find the angle that is going to give you a specific way to talk to and share with your audience so that the ones who are most likely to purchase through you are listening and purchasing.

This is true for anyone who is just starting out in business, too. If you are starting a business with the purpose of generating success online, or if you are becoming an influencer, you are going to need to find a niche so that you know who you are talking to, why, and how to reach them. This way, you are more likely to reach those individuals.

As someone who does not already have a business in place, you do face the setback of not already having statistics around who you are most likely to earn sales from, which means that you are going to have to start from scratch. However, starting fresh means that you do have the capacity to choose the niche that is most interesting to you while also having the most growth potential online, which can be an incredible opportunity to maximize your success.

If you are brand new in business, the best thing that you can do is determine what type of business model you want to follow, and then research what the latest trends are in that particular model. So, if you want to sell products or services, you need to identify what types of products or services are selling the most online. If you want to be an influencer, you need to identify what types of influencers are making the most income online. The key here is to make sure that you are looking at the right numbers. Avoid looking at industries that have the most businesses that are online, and instead look at the industries that have the most businesses *that are actually making a strong profit* online. This is how you can ensure that you are choosing a niche that is going to be lucrative in offering you great opportunities to make money, rather than choosing a niche that is going to be saturated with businesses or influencers. If it is saturated and no one is making a decent profit, there is a good chance that you are looking at a low-quality industry.

While you look at industries that are going to offer the most opportunity, make sure that you are also looking for industries that are interesting to you. Attempting to make a go at it in an industry that you do not understand or that does not interest you is going to end with you falling flat because you are not passionate enough to really give it the type of energy it needs to grow. Instead, pick one that makes you excited because that will make it far easier to help you gain the momentum that you need to grow your business rapidly and have great success with it, too.

Creating Your Profiles and Pages Properly

Choosing your niche is only part of using social media as a marketing strategy. The next part of making the most out of social media is knowing how to set your profiles and pages up properly. Online, your profiles and pages offer a sort of "store front" for people to look at, so it is crucial that you create them in a way that helps leave a positive impression of you and your business in the eyes of your visitors.

It is important that you always approach the topic of your profiles and pages with this intention of making the best first impression possible. This way, you are looking at them with the perspective required to ensure that they are sending the right message and encouraging people to follow you, trust you, and buy from you, rather than driving people away or leaving them confused or uncertain.

Every single social media platform has fairly similar features in what is available for you to customize on your profile. Typically, you can brand your profile pictures, header images, a tagline, your username, and your wall or your personal feed. These areas can be branded to leave a very specific impression of what your business stands for so that people know as soon as they look at your profile who you are and what they can expect.

In the past, it was enough to write a basic tagline and use images that showed your logo and maybe a professional headshot of you, depending on what your industry was. These days, this type of generic approach is not nearly enough to capture the attention of people and leave them thinking about you and your services over anyone else. Instead, you need to do something that sets you apart and caters directly to your niche so that they see you, remember you, and willingly come back for more. This is where knowing your personal niche is useful: you know what type of customizations and features they would appreciate. This way, you can brand and customize your profile accordingly.

For example, if you are a realtor who focuses on the niche of first-time home buyers that are also families with children, you might make your profile picture a professional headshot where you are standing in front of a nice home that is in a family-friendly neighborhood. You may also have evidence of children in the background, such as a nearby park or playground, or some children's toys in the front yard of the home. If you are an influencer who specializes in talking to country western people who love the rodeo and western style, you might make your profile picture of you well dressed in traditional western wear standing in front of a barn or some livestock. Getting the right energy into your pictures, as well as your descriptions, usernames, and captions is crucial to really set yourself apart from other people in your industry.

Identifying Winning Strategies for Marketing On Social Media

Knowing how to authenticate your chosen marketing strategies for social media is crucial if you are going to pick strategies that are actually going to help you succeed. In this day and age, countless blog posts and articles are swirling around the internet providing all sorts of information on how you can leverage social media for business growth. Unfortunately, many of these are outdated or feature strategies that have yet to be truly tested for excellent growth. If you want to grow on social media, you are going to need to identify the strategies that help you grow *rapidly* so that you waste no time in reaching the right markets with your posts.

The best way to authenticate and validate your potential strategies is to look for other people who are using them. A strong strategy that actually works will be one that is being used by many of the major accounts, particularly those which are known for staying on top of the current trends such as brands like Nike and Sephora. Do not just focus on large brands, though, as they tend to be more resilient toward less effective strategies. Look at brands that are just a bit ahead of you as well and see if they are also using those strategies with any success. If multiple brands in all levels of success are using your ideal strategy, chances are it is a great strategy that is going to work for you, as well. If, however, you are looking at a strategy and not many people are having success with it, or it seems to be avoided or not even on the radar of larger brands, it is probably not worth your while to try it out.

In addition to looking around to see who is using these strategies and how well they are succeeding with them, you also need to authenticate the quality of the source that you have received your tips from. Receiving guidance from companies that are offering a service that is meant to help you grow, for example, may be hit or miss because they may be catering to their own services in the advice that they give. In other words, they may be giving you advice that is geared specifically toward getting you to buy or use their products to help you grow. This does not mean that it is low quality advice, or that the service being offered is low quality, but it does mean that the advice could be biased. If you are looking at strategies or advice offered by companies looking to sell their products or services to help you grow, make sure that you validate what they are saying. If what they are saying is true and is working for other people online, chances are they are a reliable source to receive information from.

You can also validate what they are saying by looking at other people who have used their products or services and seeing how their growth is going. As well, look at their own social media platforms and strategies, and see how it is working for them in particular. Unfortunately, there are many companies out there who claim to have winning growth strategies yet they themselves seem to be struggling to make any growth online. If you find that a company is making claims such as having the capacity to gain you tens of thousands of followers or earn you a specific amount of money but they themselves seem to not have that same level of success on their own platforms, be wary. These types of businesses are generally making false claims and could be offering low quality advice and ineffective services that will interrupt your success and leave you struggling.

Once you have validated the quality of your possible strategies by validating the source and validating the effectiveness of each strategy, you should be able to feel confident in whether or not these are strategies that will work. If they are not strategies that will work, or if they seem unreliable or like it may be hit or miss, avoid working with that strategy. This is likely only going to waste your time. If, however, they are strategies that are working for other people and seem to be reliable in offering growth, it is worth giving them a try to see if you can make them work for you, too!

Chapter 1 Preliminary Considerations

Before we go through the different social media marketing strategies, we have to address one thing first:

Why is Traditional Marketing Failing?

And to answer this question, we have to understand the basic concept of marketing. In essence, we create advertisements that say something about a business, have it shown in any of the channels we own or pay rent for, and then hope the advertisements draw in enough people willing to become paying customers to your brand.

And so the usual sequence for traditional marketing is always this:

Person watches or listens to something.

Advertisement butts in for thirty seconds or so to tell the person about what a business is offering.

Advertisement ends and the program resumes.

Think of traditional marketing as like a horror movie jump scare. It's something that people more or less do, not expecting to interrupt the mood, and minus the scares.

However, such form of advertising through the different online media right now is suffering from the lowest possible click-through rates and the reason is quite obvious: It's invasive, interruptive, and quite so unpredictable in its appearance that your modern potential customer gets more annoyed than intrigued.

And, given the level of control one person has with the kind of information being fed to them these days, it is not too uncommon for people to tune out from these advertisements as soon as they pop up.

According to surveys, traditional marketing has been rejected by potential audiences in a number of ways, including:

- Teenagers and young adults saying that they would unsubscribe from social media channels and websites if they feature too much forced and un-skippable advertisements.

- 86% of TV viewers immediately changing channels if advertisements start appearing.

- 91% of e-mail subscribers dropping out of their subscriptions in an e-mail list if they receive too many irrelevant notifications.

With such level of discomfort being attributed to traditional forms of advertising done in the online world, it is no surprise why they are not faring well recently.

This implies that you have to create something that would resonate well with your audience the most in any social media channel that you would wish to operate in. This means that you have to mold your message to fit the format and language of every social media site out there.

And to do that, you have to understand what makes for good marketing content.

The Anatomy of Good Advertising Content

Regardless of shape and format, advertising content would always follow the same scheme. In essence, content can come in three major categories which are:

Product - This is what the advertising is offering to the audience. It is tangible and comes in the form of a purchasable item, service, or other promotion.

Role - The advertisement basically assumes a role in your audience's life. What is it trying to do for that person? What kind of problems does it solve? What type of questions is it trying to answer? Answering these questions often determines the narrative being presented by your marketing strategies.

Emotion - An ad of this type is designed to connect to the audience on an emotional, if not personal, level. The point of this content is to evoke some kind of emotional response from your audience. Or, at the very least, it tries to introduce a new kind of perspective that could change the way they regard a certain issue or problem.

So which of these content types are the best for your business? Neither. Each has its own set of strengths and weaknesses which means that focusing on one while disregarding the others is not going to do you any favors in the long run.

For instance, focusing too much on product-based content can make your advertising feel out of touch with your audience, as they don't connect to your brand on a personal level. On the flip side, if you don't have a lot of product-based advertising and too much emotional advertising, then you are not giving your audiences something tangible to anchor their loyalty to your brand.

The anatomy of a highly effective marketing strategy in social media, then, is finding a balance between all three of these categories. Simply put, your marketing must offer something tangible, introduce something that is actionable, plays a relevant role in the lives of your target audience, and can connect to them on a personal level.

Organic and Paid Marketing: Which is Which?

A common misconception with marketing is that all types of marketing content can be lumped into a single category. The truth, however, is that marketing can fall into two categories: organic and paid.

A smart business owner would use both advertising types in tandem to reach their target market and even discover new segments in the process. However, in order to do that, you have to understand what makes both advertising types different from one another.

Organic Marketing

Marketing falling under this category is best for a number of functions including:

- Establishing the style and voice of your brand.

- Educating potential audiences.

- Driving traffic to landing pages.

- Making the business an authority in a certain topic or industry.

Simply put, organic marketing is there to increase the "awareness" for your business. The cycle of organic marketing often follows the same sequence which is:

The scheduled production and publishing of content like blog posts and articles for Search Engine Optimization (SEO) purposes. The articles must be aligned to what your target market cares for the most, the problems that they face, and even issues that are being tackled in the wider industry that your business is a part of.

Sharing of these posts on social media. Again, the way that this content is shared must be in line with the format and language of that platform.

Tagging influencers and other appropriate brands in your social media posts as well as using your content in regular newsletters for subscribers.

Monitoring how the content is being consumed by the market. Analytics and other monitoring tools will become crucial in this phase, as it tells you whether or not people are engaging with your content and if your content is funneling traffic from your social media accounts to your main web pages.

If it is not obvious to you, organic marketing is focused on tactics that produce authentic and value-based reactions. In essence, if you produce something of value to your audience, you are convincing them more to convert into paying customers. And if you already have converted them into paying customers, the content you further produce will help in ensuring that they remain loyal to your business.

Paid Marketing

On the other hand, paid marketing is designed to help businesses optimize the sales conversion process. If organic marketing is there to "establish" your presence, then paid marketing is there to "push" it. Due to this, paid marketing is much more focused on sales and generating a purchase-focused action among target audiences.

How the paid marketing cycle goes is as follows:

Commissioning for the Creation of "Advertising Content." This would also include creating a schedule of when these ads are going to be published and in what sets.

Once the initial results are in for every published set, the marketing team then reviews which ads performed the best.

Some would even invest more money in improving these top-performing ads or creating new ads similar to them.

Once every quarter is complete, the marketing team then reviews data drawn from the entire marketing campaign. Things to look for are expenses, returns of investment, returns on assets, and other important metrics.

The key to success with paid marketing is to be specific with your goals in order to produce specific actions. For instance, each paid ad might be linked to a very specific page of your website such as the landing page, the sales page, or the products page.

Other specific actions you could drive with paid advertising includes:

- Improving returns on investment and assets.

- Making a specific impression on the various platforms you operate in.

- Hitting specific sales goals or, better yet, going beyond them.

- Optimizing ads in real-time.

- Testing marketing campaigns before full implementation to identify what parts make them effective (and where they might fail).

However, the most *important* metrics you have to look out for in paid advertising will include:

Conversion Rates - The traffic coming from your social media pages that not only engage with your web pages but would actually complete the sales conversion process.

Engagement - The amount of likes, shares, views, and comments that each ad generates in a period of time after being published.

Advertisement Type - The types of advertisements that had the highest rates in conversion and engagement.

Where do These Advertising Types Fit in Your Marketing Campaign?

The one thing that you have to understand is that both paid and organic marketing actually complement each other well. There are even certain aspects where both advertisement types overlap into each other which can optimize conversion rates and incoming traffic in your main web pages.

However, the truth is that both advertisement forms are rarely used in tandem due to budget concerns. Paid advertising, as the name implies, requires you to invest more in order to generate tangible results.

On the other hand, even if you have a large advertising budget, you are not going to improve on your business's sales conversion if your content does not naturally engage with your target audience.

As such, it is important that you identify where you must use paid and organic marketing either in tandem or exclusively. Some of your marketing goals will rely on one form while others can be achieved if you used either type.

Once you have found a balance between paid and organic marketing, what you must do then is to constantly test and improve on your strategies throughout the entire campaign.

Some (Harsh) Social Media Realities That You Must Face

What you have to understand is that changes in consumer behavior has not only affected traditional marketing, but even online marketing. What worked for social media sites a few years back no longer applies today.

As such, if you want to truly survive in the world of social media, you need to face some realities about the current state of affairs.

Reality #1: Brand Recognition No Longer Means as Much as It Did

Traditional marketing has always been the act of telling the rest of the world that your business is the best of whatever it is doing or, at the very least, a fairly trusted brand in the field. But how does the rest of the social media market treat that same line whenever a company says it today? Noise. Loud, unnecessary, irrelevant noise.

The harshest truth you might face with social media is that nobody on there really cares about your business. And those that swear that they support your business won't be there for long if you start making mistakes here and there.

So, if the image you create is no longer important, what then matters for social media people? The answer is one word: solutions.

Simply put, marketing today is no longer about how well-known or trusted your brand is, but how applicable your offerings are in solving actual problems. As such, those that offer the best possible solutions to a problem, and at reasonable prices, tend to be at the top.

Reality #2: It's a Free-For-All

A few years back, the only kind of competition you needed to worry about came from the companies that offered the same products/services as you, or those that targeted the same demographics. Today, competition can come in any form or size.

In most cases, the competition you should take seriously today will come from smaller companies or lesser-known people. The reason for this is that they are closer to their target markets and can keep them engaged through a mixture of organic and paid marketing schemes (more so in the former).

In fact, you will find that less popular brands and individuals can garner stronger followings while big companies like Gap, Pepsi, and Spirit Airlines have to deal with backlash after backlash from their tone deaf social media strategies.

Also, the increase of volume in competition today gives rise to the problem of information overload for target markets. The more manufactured noise that similar companies generate on social media, the more people tend to ignore what they are trying to say.

Reality #3: Philanthropy is the New Form of Marketing

In a rather odd turn of events, marketing today has taken a rather altruistic tone. And no, this does not mean that companies have forgotten that they are capitalists by heart, as they still aim to make a lot of money from the markets.

What the shift means is that more and more people respond to marketing strategies that make them feel good. And what makes people feel good right now is if companies "stand up" for the "little man."

As such, you might notice that some companies are beginning to take up a stance in social issues, political topics, and even environmental concerns. By showing that they care for the rest of the world, companies give potential customers some value of sorts.

However, there is the drawback of becoming too political or ideological with your marketing. What you have to remember is that people don't like being talked down to. Whether it is you telling them how to live or making them feel ashamed for not caring too much, you can expect a lot of blowback from the market if the message you think is noble is perceived to be pushy and abrasive.

And there are quite a lot of brands out there that overdo it with taking a stand on social issues. The key to success, then, is to temper a business's newfound altruistic side with the notion that one is in business to give people what they want.

Either way, the point is that your brand has to give something of value if you want potential customers to trust it. Otherwise, you are not going to be as relevant in the years to come which, in turn, affects your visibility in the social media arena.

What this all means is that your marketing strategies in social media are utterly dependent on how people behave on them, whether you like it or not. And understanding the behavior of the modern day potential customer is crucial for the sole reason that, in order for your strategies to be deemed successful in social media, they must complete a step-by-step process of becoming paying customers.

Chapter 2 Finding the Right Social Media Platform for Your Business

Social media marketing is a necessity for companies that seek growth. There are many platforms to choose from when deciding on where to begin. Nevertheless, below are the three steps that can aid in locating the correct social media platform to concentrate on.

Define Your Target Audience

There may be times when you might get adverts from numerous businesses that offer services that you might not need. You understand that putting your money into that company will be wasteful. An experienced individual may then deduce that it needs to employ a person who is more competent in target advertisements.

Checking important demographics like user location and gender can help you gain knowledge about your desired audience. It is also essential to figure out the social media platforms that your competitors use to interact with their customers successfully. A simple keyword search on Google is an effective way to gain insight regarding the network that your target market makes use of the most. You can, for instance, enter terms such as golf courses + Facebook or golf clubs + Pinterest. It does not matter if your brand is the type that sticks to a particular niche; you will be pleasantly astonished at the vast array of individuals that use certain social media platforms. Interacting with a non-target audience is bound to cost money with no foreseeable upside. If deciding what target audience is best for your brand is a bit challenging, answering the questions below will shed some light on how you can achieve it.

- What are your audience's average age and gender?

- What is the average income of your prospective audience?

- What is the location of your target market?

- What companies employ these individuals?

- Do they have families?

- Are they homeowners?

- Do they face any challenges that need a solution?

- Do they have hobbies or enjoyable activities?

- What avenues do they get their information from digitally or traditionally?

When all these questions are answered, you can gain valuable insight into the demographics of your target audience.

Set an Objective That You Hope to Achieve Through Social Media

Quite a lot of business owners and social media marketers tend not to have a detailed objective to show what they want to achieve using social media. They always focus on making dreams come true without a clear definition of what their goals may be. For that reason, they often end up chasing their tails, with no visible progress in sight.

If you want to make sales using social media, it is imperative to have a clear vision and take steps towards it. You should remember that the majority of social media platforms are places where people go to view content rather than do things or be sold on things. That is why you need action to accompany your words and make money from social media marketing.

State your marketing aims for social media. Is the purpose to increase your audience, interact with current customers or enhance your brand's visibility on social media? You should audit your business by first analyzing strategies currently in place for gaps. Do you also wish to expand your consumer base, improve customer service, gain shoppers' loyalty, developing a feedback avenue, inform customers about deals, services, and products, drive traffic to your site or run an informal type of market research?

Instead of defining your aims in relation to the number of followers or fans you intend to reach, you should carefully consider the platform that will increase your level of engagement with customers. That is a metric that doesn't depict business success accurately. It is necessary to note that, on social media, a bigger audience may not always convert to money-making results.

Understand B2B or B2C Operation

Is your brand more of a business-to-consumer (B2C) or business-to-business (B2B) type?[2] The reason for this question is that it isn't common for individuals to head to digital platforms when they aim to buy something. Thus, it might take quite a bit of effort and energy to grab their attention once they are on the site.

Nevertheless, active users on social media can be the best target audience. A B2B brand is more suited to platforms that enable you to advertise and reach the correct market. One of the channels that fit the bill is LinkedIn. On this site, you can post your business information and other content that may lure potential consumers towards the brand.

A B2C brand will get a lot of opportunities through the use of social media platforms like Twitter, Facebook, YouTube, and Instagram. These are platforms that enable your brand engage directly with both your existing and potential customers.

Decide on the Content Type That You Should Create

Varying content forms are more effective on particular social media sites than others. That's why it is important to consider the format that you should create. For example, Instagram is known as an image-sharing platform, so it is wrong for a brand to choose whitepapers as an advertising tool. The proper content type is generally dependent on a few variables, such as the industry, brand, and target audience. Some of the formats that are available to businesses include podcasts, blog posts, testimonials, live streams, webinars, whitepapers, e-books, photographs, and videos.

Think of Your Resources and Skills

It is common for every channel to have a unique way of engaging the audience. However, each one also requires varying resources and skill sets to be used. Hence, you should identify what they are to create and execute a social media marketing strategy on various platforms successfully.

You must ensure that your business' needs align with a specific social media site, for one. There are a lot of marketing tools available online for free as well. These can aid in content creation and optimization for every platform. Furthermore, you should think about your strengths and research what skills and resources are necessary to remain active on such channels.

Selecting the correct platform and picking a marketing plan that fits your business is integral to save resources and time down the line.

Connect Your Audience, Goals, and Content Using the Appropriate Platform

Comparing the numerous social media sites to help you figure out which one can supply your brand's requirements the most is the next step after deciding on your goals, content type, and target audience. Below is a brief rundown of the popular platforms, what they provide, and what an average user on the platform is like:

Facebook

Facebook is the biggest networking site out there with more than 2 billion users actively using it every month.[3] As a social media platform, it is great for generating leads. It has an advertising feature as well, which can be used to customize ads for specific audiences. When it comes to building relationships, humanizing your business, and creating loyal customers from leads, Facebook is the right place to be. Like Twitter, it is capable of reaching quite a large amount of people, but it also means that you have a lot of competition here.

LinkedIn

This is the go-to option for business-to-business brands, particularly for those with lead generation as their primary goal. It is also a fantastic platform to house editorial content, which is useful for cementing your company's place as an industry leader that can be trusted to create brand value and authority while engaging leads via interactive conversations. LinkedIn has a demographic that is different from those on other sites, considering many users are typically between 30 and 49 years old.

Pinterest

When it comes to Pinterest, images are of the utmost importance. It is a great channel for entrepreneurs who intend to increase sales since many account holders make or plan purchases there. Pinterest has a more significant number of women compared to men, too, and is usually full of graphics.[4] After all, it offers creative categories such as décor, art, food, fashion, travel, wedding, et cetera that businesses may contribute to by posting beautiful photographs.

Twitter

Twitter is the type of networking site that asks users to provide rapid responses to others. It is the go-to site as well for company that wants to quickly reach followers with its announcements, breaking news, and relevant messages. The majority of Twitter users are aged under 50, and the best format to work on is textual since it can be easily digested into quotations, listicles, and how-to articles. Pictures tend to fare better on the site compared to videos as well.

Making Your Facebook Usage a Success

As one of the most used social media platforms in the world, more people understand Facebook's functionality and reach. If you are able to understand the channel's quirks, it opens up many possibilities. The question is, "Is there a way to make this platform work for you?" Below are some ways to achieve it.

Ensure That It Has a Touch of Humanity

When you personalize interactions with your followers, you can earn their trust. You have to create posts that employ a first-person, conversational tone. Page administrators have to show their names and pictures, too. When this is done, it results in increased brand loyalty as well as closer relationships.

Don't Miss Out on Using Facebook Ads

Assuming your page is not doing too poorly, it entails that your followers have grown to like your brand. You can even expand your viewership organically since your current fans are highly engaged with your content and consistently share your post with others. Nevertheless, if you aren't patient enough to wait, you may make your page more famous via advertisements.

You can get new visitors by creating sponsored stories and ads that target people who don't follow you yet. This way, you may encourage individuals with particular interests to like your brand's page.

It doesn't make sense to beat yourself up when only a paltry number of your followers see an important post. It is a reality that all business owners need to embrace. The way to combat a downfall is to promote your content more. Spend a bit of money on increasing your reach; do not get restricted by utilizing only the times your audience is online. You should see promoted posts as a way to maximize your engaged audience.

Let Your Branding Be Unique

You should offer an accustomed experience to your followers. It is essential to ensure that your page stands out from the rest. You should also make full brand information available on your profile, as well as related images and logos. It might be necessary to create bespoke features and applications that highlight your business theme, too.

Promote Interaction Between Your Customers

You have to be proficient enough to get on your consumers' good side. Customers already talk to each other, so it makes sense to take advantage of this fact to minimize costs while actively enhancing the customer experience. To be specific, highlight the contribution of loyal fans and ensure that the top contributors are recognized on your wall. This engagement can be further encouraged by creating a discussion board using Facebook's provided feature.

Find Ways to Promote Word-of-Mouth

Word of mouth is still the most effective marketing form.[5] Prospective clients tend to see fellow customers to speak more reliably about a brand than its employees or even the owner. Most people are usually swayed to make use of a service or product because a person they know has previously done it. What you need to do, therefore, is to ask current customers to share and recommend your page to others, like your posts or share your links.

Make and Mark Milestones

Looking at your brand's milestones is a great way to tell your story. Creating benchmarks helps to inform your followers how much progress your business has made. You can incorporate images to ensure these stories are much more interactive than others, too, and fans can know your humble beginnings. You can be as creative as you can with every milestone.

Have a Proper Plan for Creating and Publishing Posts

Developing a posting schedule is useful for Facebook Insights. Using this tool ensures that you can observe and schedule the best times to publish content. This is especially beneficial if your audience is in a different timezone, and you are unavailable during the particular hours when your audience expects content from you.

Using the Pin Option for Pertinent Information

An issue that most people have when using Facebook for marketing purposes is the fact that they create a post that gets only a minimal amount of visibility and ends up buried within the timeline. However, you can resolve it by sticking that content to the top of the page. Once you do so, you can ensure that the post is available right at the beginning. It lasts for as much as seven days.

Provide a Call to Action

Make sure to provide a call to action. Numerous brands tend to commit the mistake of not creating a one that seamlessly drives fans right from interacting with the page to purchasing something. Its purpose is to increase the numbers of products or services sold.

A call to action can be instantaneous but straightforward. It should be posted on the landing page and your brand's Facebook wall. You may ask your fans to register for emails or newsletters while they like and share the page as well. Current followers and prospective customers should be redirected to tabs that allow them to view products, check out exclusive deals, and avail your offerings.

Organize Contests

Organizing a contest can help you invest in your fanbase and generate publicity. For your content to run properly, it has to be actively engaged. Every moment a person enters your page's contest, a story, which their friend can view, get created. Additionally, it is essential to set it up in a manner that only current followers can participate.

Engage in Conversations

Connections can be made with prospective clients by actively encouraging interaction that goes both ways. These types of conversations increase communication, passing of information, and trust. When followers leave comments, it is important to reply to them and offer individual rewards. It is also advisable to publicly thank your followers for supporting your brand.

The moment you start a direct conversation with a customer, it actively reaches their network. Each time a follower comments on a brand's Facebook page, the conversation becomes shared among a minimum of 100 friends since an average number of friends is 338 friends for a Facebook user.[6]

Discover the beautiful work of social media for business; ensure that you are not missing out on the opportunities it offers by opening an account on a suitable social media channel.

Chapter 3 Integrating Social Media into Your Omnichannel Marketing Strategy

The advent of the internet has brought profound changes in the world today. It can be argued that the internet has given a huge boost to technological innovations. Today, there are numerous devices that people can use to purchase products over the internet. Their shopping experience is even made more convenient since they can order products from their social media pages and collect these goods from physical stores. What this means is that the shopping experience for customers has been transformed as they not only find it convenient to shop using social media apps, but they also fancy the idea that products are closer to them than ever before. Omnichannel marketing strategy centers around the idea of providing clients with a seamless and integrated shopping experience in all the marketing channels used by a particular company.

The competitive nature of businesses today should influence companies to strive and meet customer demands without bias. In this case, it doesn't matter where a customer is shopping, what matters is that they get the products that they purchased online. This means that businesses should work to seamlessly integrate both online and physical stores. For an optimal omnichannel experience, it is imperative that social platforms should also be integrated to work harmoniously. Ultimately, this leads to a huge boost in consumer engagement.

Today, we have seen businesses benefit from the fact that they are integrating social media marketing into other marketing channels that they are using. The best part is that these businesses win over the hearts and minds of their customers. In the real sense, if a customer finds it convenient to shop from their phone and get the products delivered to a physical store that they can easily access, there is a good chance that they will shop more. On the contrary, single-channel customers will not be as motivated to shop as those who have experienced the benefits of omnichannel marketing.

Digitally speaking, omnichannel customers are more proficient in the way in which they use their devices to shop. Interestingly, they are also more willing to spend compared to customers who have not been through an omnichannel experience. Often, omnichannel clients can engage anywhere and still purchase products. For that reason, it is vital that businesses should obtain and integrate insights that they get from multi-channel analytics and from their social media marketing. This is the best way to deliver exceptional customer experience that will also benefit them in the long run.

An important fact that should be made clear about the integration of omnichannel marketing with social media is that price is not a factor that influences people's shopping habits. If retailers ignore their customers and fail to place importance on their shopping experience, there is a good chance they will suffer. People will want to depend on a brand that provided them with a great shopping experience regardless of the price tags on their products/services. So, blending social media marketing with an omnichannel marketing strategy has little to do with price.

What is Omnichannel Marketing?

Maybe you are still racking your brain trying to figure out what omnichannel marketing means. This refers to a marketing approach which brings together varying communication channels used by businesses to reach their customers. Businesses use customer interests and perspectives on brands or specific products and services to optimize their marketing messages. Ultimately, this helps them to maintain consistency in all their marketing channels. The result of this is that it increases the effectiveness of marketing campaigns.

There are numerous ways in which we have enjoyed an omnichannel experience. In the banking industry, for example, there are certain banks which have taken steps to ensure that their customers can enjoy all their services from the convenience of their mobile application. In this case, you can easily schedule appointments as well as deposit a check without having to visit the bank in person. The same can be done for payment of bills and other monthly expenses.

In addition, there are loyalty programs offered by brands as a way of enticing their prospects and loyal customers. Usually, these programs are simply incentives which are meant to motivate people to purchase more of a particular product or depend on a certain service. Such exciting shopping experience gives a customer a reason to maintain their loyalty with a particular brand.

Tips to Successfully Integrate Social Media into Your Omnichannel Marketing Strategy

To guarantee that you maximize the benefits that come with blending social media into your omnichannel marketing strategy, the following points should be considered.

Engage in Social Listening

An effective way of knowing your customers on social media is by engaging in social listening. This gives you the opportunity to find out exactly where they engage with their friends on social media pages. That's not all, you will also gain insight on conversations about your industry and your brand. Analyzing the insights that you get on your customers helps you meet customer expectations as you will deliver just what they are looking for. Keeping this in mind, adding in what you learn from social listening will undeniably enhance both your products and service provision in all the marketing channels you use.

Mixing Social Media and Email Marketing

Bringing together social media and email marketing can also be a great strategy to boost engagement in your marketing campaign. How do you do this? You should consider promoting your social media pages using email. Here, you should encourage your customers to get more information about your brand by visiting your social media profiles. Remember, you should make this easy for them by adding social media buttons on the emails you send.

The same marketing strategy can also be adopted on your social media pages. Your posts should encourage people by offering them freebies once they opt to sign up for your newsletters.

Centralize the Data Collected

Social media pages provide you with a wide array of information about your customers. This means that you can make good use of this information to personalize your promotional messages. Besides knowing more about your clients' tastes and preferences, you are also informed about their hobbies, shopping habits, health perceptions, and lifestyle choices, etc.

With all the information that you get from your clients, it is crucial that you create a complete profile featuring your specific target audience. This is where the use of customer relationship management (CRM) software comes in handy. With the help of this tool, you can gather and centralize your customer information. The advantage gained here is that your social media team can work harmoniously across different social media platforms.

Never Ignore Your Audience

The last thing that you should do to your prospects is ignore them. This is something that you might be tempted to do more so when they are responding negatively to your social media posts. Ignoring these negative messages will not solve anything. It is vital that you respond to everything on your social media account. This is what engagement is all about.

Your team should be well-trained to use tools that help monitor all conversations relating to your brand. This is the best way to not miss out on anything which could tarnish your brand's image.

Support In-App Purchases

An exceptional strategy to providing your clients with an omnichannel experience is by merging your business website to your social networks. This gives your prospects and customers the ability to purchase products through their social networks. Your clients do not need to necessarily visit your business website to make purchases. Integrated links on your social media posts will automate the process for them.

Encourage Recommendations

People will want to buy your products if there are recommendations from friends in their social circle. For that reason, you should encourage testimonials from other customers who have used your product/service. Don't make it difficult for customers to tell other people about their shopping experience with your brand. Include convenient share buttons after completing transactions. This way, they will find sharing easy as they only need to make a few clicks to recommend your brand in their social circles. The same case applies if you prefer to give your customers an opportunity to leave their feedback. Aim to make the process easy for them.

Cross-Channel Social Media Marketing with Marketing Automation

Technology has indeed brought about numerous changes in the way people communicate. People always strive to be connected using social media. It is therefore not surprising to find people interacting on their social media profiles and checking their emails throughout the day. We have smartphones to help us remain connected and help us stay up to date with what is happening around us. In fact, the use of smartphones has become a norm even in the workplace and most social settings.

Businesses have to face the challenge of penetrating through all the noise and delivering their messages to their intended prospects and customers. Now, this is where cross-channel social media marketing comes in. This refers to a marketing approach where brands find an effective way of seamlessly communicating with their prospects and customers across multiple channels.

Through this marketing approach, there are several benefits that they could gain. Some of these are succinctly discussed in the following paragraphs.

Before getting into detail concerning the benefits of cross-channel social media marketing, it is important to understand that this approach is different from multi-channel marketing. Most people will confuse the two terms and therefore, it is essential that you draw a line between the two.

A multi-channel marketing approach concerns the idea of having an online presence on several channels. In this case, brands can have an online presence using a mobile application and a business website. On the contrary, a cross-channel strategy refers to an approach where brands provide their customers with a seamless experience on all the different channels that they are using to market their brand.

A good example of how this works is when customers use the internet to research brands and products that they can rely on. Often, brands will find a way of reaching these customers through email applications on their smartphones. Therefore, there is a continuous experience that a shopper will experience as brands move from one channel to another without actually interrupting the customer. Some of the pros of this form of marketing strategy include:

Increasing Engagement

Cross-channel social media marketing with marketing automation will often lead to an increase in the engagement levels between brands and their customers. The idea of using multiple marketing channels to reach customers means that you will be interacting with them throughout the day. For instance, when customers are accessing their emails and updating their social accounts. Brands remain connected with their prospects in all the stages of their purchasing cycle. Therefore, it would be easy to remind a consumer that they did not complete a particular purchase they were interested in.

Enhanced Loyalty

The consistency that a cross-channel marketing approach offers gives customers an easier way of reaching out to brands. This is because they are always kept updated with new products/services that brands are planning to introduce to the market. Discounts and other product information which could benefit them are some of the things that they are always informed about. Consequently, such interaction could drive customers to become loyal to a particular brand.

Chapter 4 The Sales Conversion Process

Although marketing might sound complicated, it actually follows a rather simple and straightforward sequence. Here's the catch, though: Any member of your audience could be in either of these stages currently.

The 4 Stages: How a Prospect Becomes a Paying Customer

You have to know in what stage of the conversion process your audience is in to craft a message that would resonate with them well. So, how does one person go from an absolute stranger to your business to a loyal customer?

They do so in 4 steps.

1. *Attraction*

Since this is the start of the process, you can expect it to be the more labor-intensive phase compared to subsequent ones. This is where any business would have to introduce people to their products/services and give them the assurance that whatever they are paying for is good.

Of course, since this is the start of the process, the target audience at this phase absolutely does not know anything about the business. As such, the goal here is to inform and educate them by answering their queries. Visibility is a major factor in this phase which is why it is recommended that you adopt a rather aggressive strategy, especially if your business is relatively new to the world of social media.

2. *Conversion*

Once your social media pages are funneling traffic to your web pages, the focus shifts from introducing them to the brand to turning them into potential leads. Here, you may have to rely on your web pages' design and even the presentation of your content to give the push that your leads need to complete the conversion process. You should also have set up systems in your pages where you can easily retarget these people at a later date.

However, your social media pages will still play a crucial role in this part. Through your channels, you can offer them something of value like discounts and promises of access to high-end content if they subscribe or register to your brand.

However, don't go straight for a "hard sell" by immediately offering them all of your available products or services, as you want them to get to know your business more first.

In other words, the goal here is to entice the leads so they would stay on your pages long enough, and make them trust you to the point that they will trade their basic information for something that they can find value with.

3. *Closing*

Once you have your leads, the goal then is to turn these people into paying customers. Since you already have their basic information, retargeting your leads should be fairly straightforward now. Once you have a pool of potential leads to your site via those subscriptions to your social media profiles, you can provide them with even better offers so they would initiate the sales process.

This can be the most demanding part of the sales conversion cycle as you are now aiming to convince people to part with their money to try out something that you are offering. The chances of people bailing on the process is quite high at this part but those that are sufficiently convinced with your marketing at this point will have increased chances of closing a deal with you.

At this point, you can only rely on the quality of your marketing strategies in the first two phases as well as the ones you are publishing at this phase. If they are quite good, people will not only initiate a transaction with the business but would actually go through the entire process, resulting in a sale.

4. *Delighting*

Most business are content with turning one visitor into a paying customer. After all, the sales conversion process is technically complete. However, it would be better if you maintain a relationship with satisfied customers.

Once the main sales process is complete, the next phase will involve enticing these customers with even more offers. The goal for your marketing at this point is to give people a reason to come back to your channels.

The reason for this is quite simple: There is no better endorser to your business than people who actually tried your offerings and found them to be good. If all of your subsequent offerings live up to the promises in your marketing, you can establish a loyal customer base which will promote your business for you in their own little ways.

Nurturing Your Leads

Let's assume that you mastered the art of converting strangers into loyal customers and you know of strategies that can quickly drum up interest for your brand. So now, you have quite a lot of traffic going from your social media pages to your main website.

However, there is still one problem that you would have to face: Not all of those visitors actually become customers. In fact, the people that actually convert into customers coming from your social media pages don't even comprise 20% of your site's day-to-day traffic.

So why aren't visitors actually making important purchasing decisions when on your social media pages? The answer is simple:

Not Everyone Who Clicks Through Your Content is Ready to Make a Purchase

You could focus on generating leads all you want. But if you want to see noticeable changes in your traffic and conversion rates, you'll have to nurture your potential leads.

One key aspect here is that you must understand that each potential lead has their own story to tell. As such, they should be handled in different ways to make them convert into customers and then free promoters.

To perform lead nurturing properly, there are a few things that you have to keep in mind:

1. Know What They Need

As was stated, not every lead is the same. Because of this, your business has to directly interact with them to understand in what phase of the conversion process they currently fall into. Have they just discovered your business? From what social media pages did they come from? Have they filled out one of your forms or subscribed to one of your channels?

Knowing where they currently are in the conversion process will give you an idea if they are ready to try out what you are offering or not. However, just remember that just because a lead is not yet ready to make that final step towards conversion now does not mean that they won't do so in the near future.

Chapter 5 The Need for High-Quality Content

What Is a High-Quality Content?

A combination of information in a graphical, audio, written or video format that appears on a website or a page is what we refer to as content. It encompasses the sourcing and presentation of data to your audience on a specific platform as well.

The type of content that qualifies as a high-quality content will vary depending on the individual. That may talk about your products and services, photos, videos, articles, blog posts, and information pages. Nonetheless, there are certain factors that you can use to assess the quality of the content. These factors include the relevance of the content to your audience, links (internal and external), grammar, formatting, reviews, and readability.

Why Is It Important for Business Growth?

Numerous benefits are available to business owners, thanks to content creation. When creating content to publish on a page, group, or website, they can promote various products extensively, for one. The DIY content creation allows them to be flexible with the content that they upload as well.

Another critical aspect is understanding what differentiates appearance from quality. The appearance is usually essential when offering a page that is simple to use and convenient for your visitors. The likelihood that a guest will become a regular on your account is determined by the quality of content you have to offer.

Here are some criteria that you should meet before being able to claim that you got a high-quality content.

- It should not solely focus on following guidelines that will merely improve SEO rankings.

- Citing the sources should be included along with the use of valid research for credibility.

- It should have valuable information, as well as unique aspects of a website, product, service or business that you are running.

- It should undergo editing and proofreading to eliminate misspellings, typographical mistakes, and grammatical errors.

- The content should align with the expectations, needs, and wants of your audience.

The type of content and topic may lead to variations during your presentation. Regardless, the objective you intend to achieve with each content should remain the same. With a high-quality content, you can choose to have multiple objectives that allow you to improve engagement, enhance brand loyalty, and promote awareness.

When you consider the short and long-term outcomes of advertising, high-quality content is more beneficial to both your business page and websites. It often falls within a category that's known as "evergreen content" since they remain relevant even years after getting uploaded.

If you are still thinking of reasons why you need high-quality content, here are further reasons to think about now.

It Improves the Usability of Your Business Website and Page

Various factors can affect the usefulness of a site. In addition to the structure of a page or website, navigation, content accessibility, and ease of use, the content quality also matters. If you have content that has excellent internal links, it will become effortless for your users to get the information they need from your page or website.

Certain businesses cannot retain online visitors because the latter can hardly find relevant information there. The problem has to do with poor internal linking. Users want a direct link to the posts that they want to see. If they must click more than three times to find one, then you shouldn't expect them to subscribe to you.

Proper use of internal linking on high-quality content will connect different contents that contain information that your users will find relevant to the topic of interest. It is usually easier to implement if you run a blog or website for your business.

If you are writing a review on a particular product, for instance, you can add an internal link. It will redirect visitors to the main product page in case they intend to make a purchase. In an instructional article, internal linking can be an excellent way to redirect readers to the videos section of the blog or website.

In the examples above, the first use of the internal link eliminates the need for the customer to search for the product page by themselves while the second example provides a video that can the customer quickly grasp the concept you are trying to describe.

Similarly, you can link any post or video from anywhere on the internet if you feel that it will be relevant to your audience. A site that is easy to navigate and has links to relevant pages enhances usability and increases user experience. The visitors that want to share your content will also be happy to find a share button after the content. It eliminates the need for copying the URL and pasting it on another platform.

Your Customers Receive Value From the Content

Whenever you run a page or website, you always need to look for ways to outdo the competition. It doesn't matter how unsaturated the niche may be; there will still be many businesses, pages, and websites trying to win over the target audience. If you want to hold on to your viewers, you need content that provides value. That will make them interested in your business industry and may help you generate ideas. Your content will also seem valuable if it can provide relevant information and answers regarding some of the hot topics in your niche.

When your visitors start finding value when reading your content, it becomes easier for them to share it with others. In this case, you are looking for information that your audience needs and giving it to them.

It Has a Longer Lifespan

As discussed earlier, some content fall into the evergreen category. They remain relevant for months and sometimes years. With such high-quality creations, your page or website will keep attracting new visitors even if you don't post for a while.

The formats that usually become evergreen content include instructional or how-to videos, case studies, and top reviews. The topic will also play a vital role in its ability to last long.

A top-ten review of the best smartphones, for instance, will not stay in the circulation as much as an article on how to select the best smartphone. The release of new mobile devices will make the phones listed in the first article outdated as the years go by. On the other hand, the general features of a phone like the RAM size, camera, screen size, and so on remain the same. The how-to guide will show the features your customers need to assess to get the best gadget.

Creating evergreen content will not be as difficult as you may think. You can follow the steps below to create one for the first time.

- Follow the best search engine optimization (SEO) practices.

- Don't include information that is date- or event-specific. Avoid adding a timestamp as well.

- You should update content regularly.

- The content should consist of a broad range of topics relating to the industry in its discussion.

- You should provide value and eliminate grammatical errors.

Although evergreen content is quite beneficial, you need to achieve a balance when posting them. While a review may not remain useful for a long time, it still falls within the expectations and needs of your customers. Striking the right balance will attract new people and keep your audience coming back.

Chapter 6 How to Structure Your Social Media Team

With over 2 billion people active on social media, it shows that your business stands to benefit by having an active social media presence. Social media channels including Facebook, Instagram, Twitter, LinkedIn, YouTube, and Snapchat provide you with a wide market to target in your marketing campaign. Marketing your brand on these social media pages isn't just about posting content and responding to your followers. Besides posting information to these accounts, you also need to manage your marketing campaign. This entails knowing what to post and the right platforms to use. More importantly, it also centers around working with the right social media team.

The structure of your social media team will have an impact on your business' success or failure. This section takes a look at some of the most important considerations when structuring your team.

Evaluate Your Current Situation

A crucial step that you ought to take before doing anything else is to ponder on your current situation. This is because there are a number of factors which will have an impact on the decisions you will be making. Your budget, for example, will influence the number of people you will choose to hire. Additionally, this will affect the social media marketing tools that you will utilize.

You should also spend some time evaluating the team that you currently have. A small company will want to cut on its overcall costs by using their current team if they are qualified to handle certain tasks. What's more, going over the resources that you can use in your marketing campaign can help a lot in knowing what you need to successfully conduct a marketing campaign.

Creating a Social Media Governance Board

You will want to have a team of professionals capable of delivering their best concerning the social media marketing project at hand. In addition to this, you should think about creating a governance board. This is a board which comprises of stakeholders and executives who oversee the whole marketing campaign. Their job is to make sure that everything runs smoothly and according to the company's goals. In your absence, they should provide directives to ensure that challenging situations are properly dealt with.

The following are pointers to help you in creating a social media governance board.

Determining the Governance Members

The first step towards creating a social media governance board is to determine who you want to serve here. Regardless of the fact that you might have people who are qualified in various ways, it doesn't guarantee that they are the right fit. Your selection should be based on key people in your social media marketing strategy. The main thing that you will be looking for here is people with the ability to foster the right direction in your marketing campaign. Some individuals you can include here are content managers, executives, directors, etc.

Create a Board Charter

After coming up with a list of people who will be serving in the governance board, your next move should be to schedule a meeting with them. During this meeting, you should discuss the goals and missions of the governance board. The outcome of your meeting would be the creation of fundamental principles that govern this board. Roles and responsibilities should also be a topic of discussion in this meeting. Generally, the significance of this meeting is to make sure that every board member knows what they should do to enhance productivity in your company.

Clarify Social Media Goals

Once the board members are made aware of their respective duties and responsibilities, the next thing is to clarify strategic social media goals. Here, the focus will be on determining the current social performance of the company and the marketing direction that it will be taking.

Break up the Project into Stages

There are varying social media marketing techniques that companies can use to reach their goals. Nonetheless, it is a prudent idea to breakdown the process into stages. The significance of this strategy is that it makes the marketing campaign easy to handle. So, instead of posting content on various social networks, it is a brilliant idea to divide the whole marketing campaign into stages.

Communicating Goals and Training Staff

The governance board is responsible for communicating the social media goals to training staff on how the set goals can be achieved. As the business owner, you should be there to meet with the board members and discuss more on the social media goals. You want to be on the same page with these stakeholders which means that your presence is of great importance.

Once you are sure that your governance board is ready, the next thing should be to communicate to the rest of your social media team. Other employees should also be trained on how they will be operating. This includes knowing where they should seek clarification whenever they feel stuck.

Your governance board should not forget the importance of meeting regularly to evaluate the company's progress with regard to set goals. Depending on the size of your team, these meetings can be scheduled weekly or monthly.

Staffing Considerations

There is a lot to consider when creating your social media team. Most new social media marketers will jump to the conclusion that one should only take into consideration the qualifications of your new team members. While this is an important factor to think about, it is not the only thing that you will be examining when putting together your social media team. Other factors that will influence your staffing are discussed below.

Budget for New Employees

Your new staff budget will definitely affect the number of people that you will be recruiting. If you are running on a tight budget, you will have to settle for a few employees capable of meeting your social media goals.

You should never focus on looking for cheaper hires because of the limited budget you have. Undeniably, this will only push you to settle for less. Moreover, it increases the likelihood of going for the wrong people. Therefore, strive to hire fewer people who are qualified instead of trying to save money by looking for people who are underqualified.

Strategic Goals

The strategic goals of your social media campaign will have a huge impact on the people you will be choosing to work on your social media campaign team. In most cases, this will affect your team's size. The bigger the goals you are looking to accomplish, the bigger your team should be. Moreover, if your company places high regard for the importance of social media marketing, then there is a good chance that you will want a big team.

Skills Required

When choosing members for your social media team, you should consider the skills that you are looking for in your marketing team. Some of the positions that you should fill when making your team selection include:

- Social Media Manager

An individual taking on this role will be responsible for creating a social media marketing strategy. For a small company, a social media manager will take on most of the responsibilities regarding social media including coordinating social media accounts, social listening, publishing content, and responding to comments.

- Content Creators

Content creators will also form an integral part of your social media team. These are the people who will work to make sure that content posted resonates with your target audience. In addition, their responsibility will be to deliver quality content that could easily encourage the audience to like, share, or retweet. Considering the fact that content is king in your social media campaign, you shouldn't ignore the importance of hiring content creators.

- Community Manager

Another crucial member of your team will be the community manager. The role of this person is to engage with your target audience. This means that they should be there to resolve any negative publicity related to your brand. Their efforts will be required to make certain that social media engagement is given a boost.

- Analyst

Evaluating your social media performance will contribute a lot to the success of your business. Often, this is made possible by using performance metrics such as traffic, engagement rates, conversions, shares etc. If you lack the required skills to track and understand how performance can be improved, then you should not forget to hire someone to do the job.

Social Media Platforms to be Used

Once you have determined the people that you will be working with, you should also take a moment to think about the platforms that you will be using. Certainly, there are tons of social media networks out there. It is crucial that you settle for the best fit for your business.

In line with choosing the most appropriate platform for your business demands, marketers might end up concluding that they should have more members to oversee different social media accounts. Sure, this might appear as a desirable move. However, there are problems that you could face including collaboration issues and consistency in your brand's voice. Accordingly, hiring more people to help you manage the different social media profiles you have is not always a wise strategy.

Fortunately, there are several social media management applications which can be used to reduce the management workload by bringing together social media profiles on one platform.

Content Strategy

The content strategy that you will adopt will also have an impact on your staffing decisions. If you are going to create high-quality content, it means that you will have to consider hiring experts for the job. Creation of videos, for example, is quite demanding. If you don't have the required skills to create interesting videos, then it is likely that people will not like your content. Therefore, as part of creating a good social media team, you have to hire skilled individuals to create the quality content that you are looking for.

Choosing the structure of your social media team will depend a lot on what you think works for your company. Regardless, there are a number of responsibilities that you should remember to cover. First, your social media team should align with the company's overall goals. It is also vital that you clarify the social media marketing objectives with your team. That's not all - social channel optimization and the content strategy to be utilized should be clearly defined for the team to work effectively. Without a plan, it will be difficult for you to coordinate campaign activities meant to promote your brand on social media. More importantly, social analytics will come in handy as they ensure that you know whether you are performing well or not.

Chapter 7 Facebook Marketing

Facebook is made for one thing — influencing people to buy your brand, and subsequently, your product. What you sell on Facebook is not your product, but your brand. Your brand is everything that is built around your product — the kind of service, connection to the brand and company name, and the lifestyle you want to portray. People don't buy products anymore simply out of usefulness; they buy products that can add to their sense of being. So, what you need to sell to people are the lifestyle they associate with the product. If buying a product will make them feel like they're part of a trend or, say, helping the environment, they are more likely to engage with your brand. When people look to buy an expensive bag or perfume, what they expect along with it is a luxurious buying experience that makes them feel fancy and cared for.

Of course, not everyone can just open an expensive store and serve champagne to make people feel like, in buying this product, they are buying an entryway into a more prestigious lifestyle. What you can do, though, is create a similar experience through Facebook — which allows you to not only connect with your users on a personal level, but also to study their interests and likes to develop your product experience accordingly. In a way, Facebook is better for selling than regular shops, because of the constant communication and feedback between the customer and the seller. What you need to do to extend the reach of your product is to take this opportunity to study your customer base and create a Facebook Page that not only attracts customers because of the product, but because of brand association.

Brand association and its creation through Facebook is invaluable for your business, because products are replaceable. Perhaps somebody else is selling the same thing, and maybe even at a cheaper rate. The only way to gain a competitive advantage in such a situation is to make people feel more included in your selling process. People buy on the basis of trust, so you must personalize yourself for them.

Showing that you care about the community you are selling in, along with creating relatability by latching on to ongoing trends and culture, is the best way to make people feel that they should exclusively buy your product. It is no secret that Facebook is the most popular social networking website in the world. Over the years, Facebook managed to evolve into an advertising tool for companies, and now plays host to several businesses that use it as a platform to promote their business. Facebook for business is now not just a fad, but a very lucrative concept that more and more companies are identifying with, and incorporating, to avail multiple benefits.

On the face of it, social media marketing is mostly free. However, it takes a sizeable amount of effort to learn how to make the most of this free tool. Of course, that's why this book is so necessary.

Basics Skills for Facebook Marketing

Although most business owners have heard about the powerful effects of social media marketing, few are confident in using it to benefit their businesses. Facebook is not designed to automatically lead you down the path of profitability. No, you need to discover that knowledge yourself. I can help you understand what to post and how to post it in order to move your fans to buy your products. Along the line, you'll learn some key skills that will help your business gain traction in the marketplace. Here are some basics skills that outline everything you need to know about Facebook marketing:

Complete and long-term commitment to Facebook marketing:

The more you understand about how social media marketing works, the easier it will be to commit to using it. And this is a long-term commitment; you don't immediately arrive with a fully-developed Facebook marketing campaign, replete with a page that has a huge, vocal following that draws in and converts customers. It's a continual process involving ongoing self-education. You'll be actively tweaking your marketing approach to stay up-to-date with trends and to take advantage of current events. The Facebook application itself is continually evolving, adding functionality that a savvy marketer can take advantage of to keep one's business on the cutting edge of success.

Understand how social media marketing works:

You'll want to learn how basic marketing principles apply to social media marketing. You'll be discovering how you can implement effective strategies to build a successful Facebook marketing campaign. This goes far beyond just setting up a profile, presenting product images with attractive descriptions, and hoping people find your new site. You'll be discovering some specific strategies used by successful Facebook marketers and learning how to apply them to your business situation.

Turn your fans and followers into loyal customers:

Regardless of how many followers or fans a business has, it doesn't automatically translate into sales. You'll be discovering skills that will help you transform interested individuals into loyal customers.

Understanding the psychology behind buyer behavior:

You'll need to learn what lies behind a customer's decision to buy a product or service. Armed with this knowledge, you can more easily design effective marketing campaigns on Facebook.

Set clear goals for marketing on Facebook:

As you gain a clear image of what can be accomplished through social media marketing, you will be able to establish specific objectives for what you want to see happen and apply practical marketing strategies to get you there.

Learn to capture and convert leads:

Discover what leads look like on Facebook and how you can trap and develop them into paying customers.

Establish reasonable expectations:

Discover what Facebook can and cannot do for you. Learn how to incorporate Facebook marketing activities into your daily routine, as well as your future planning activities.

Learn how to attract the right audience:

With any business, your marketing plan involves knowing your target audience and how to reach it. Once you know these basic principles, you then need to learn how to apply them to the medium of Facebook.

Know how to get a bigger audience:

Most businesses need a sizeable audience to make any type of impact. While engagement is important, that engagement comes from your pool of followers. You'll need to know how to increase the size of this pool to boost the amount of engagement.

Learn to function proactively:

You can't just assume that visitors to your site will press the "like" or "follow" button. Unfortunately, this rarely happens. Learn how to give your visitors a good reason to follow your business.

Learn what to promote:

Social media marketing is not about pushing products; it's about developing trust. Learn how to shift your focus to trust building, and you'll end up selling more products.

Learn how to post effectively:

This can be a little tricky. If you post too frequently, you'll annoy your followers or even be classified as spam. If you post too seldom, you'll not be seen at all. You also need to know what kind of content is most helpful to post and what to stay away from.

The purpose of this section is to help you understand how Facebook works, how Facebook for Business works, and the wonderful things you can do with the platform to reach out to potential buyers and influence them into purchasing your products or services.

Facebook Apps

Facebook is also available on mobile, and can easily be downloaded from the app store. The user interface is extremely friendly and will help you navigate through the different aspects of a typical page. Most people prefer to check the news feed available to them on their homepage and remain updated with the various developments.

Facebook has a number of applications that can be useful for anyone running a social media business portfolio. These applications were made for the sole reason of helping businesses create a strong social media presence.

Facebook Groups is one such application. You can create a Facebook group for your product, business, or just your staff. The main purpose of this application is to manage groups easily; it can be slightly difficult to manage multiple groups. You can review all the posts and interact with the members, and you don't have to open your Facebook app every time for this. Further, you can sort out the notifications for groups because groups tend to spam a lot; this way, you can keep your Facebook id and group-related business separate.

The second app is called Facebook Page Manager — a must for anyone trying to increase the reach of his or her page. Managing a page is not simple and requires a lot of work; it can be hard to deal with page-related issues on the regular app. Page Manager has a brilliant and easy-to-use interface that is perfect for anyone managing a page from their phone. It allows you to customize your page, adjust settings, or address many other issues from your phone, meaning with this app, you can work on the go.

Apps for Business Marketing

There are various apps that every Facebook marketer must have in order to be more successful. These apps are not officially made by Facebook but are meant to help you in running a business page on the platform by providing help with the content on your page and even with tracking progress.

These apps are fairly straightforward, and they are a must-have for anyone who is running the Facebook page for a business.

Custom Tab Apps

These are the kind of apps that help you to install a small website on your Facebook page. You can have customized videos, images, and other content on a single tab with the help of these apps. Not everybody has brilliant editing and computer skills; if you are one of those people, these apps will do that work for you, allowing you to offer your customers everything that they might need. Recommendations: Hayo and Tabsite.

Email capture apps

These are the apps that will help you capture the email addresses of your Facebook audience without disturbing them. It can be really difficult to get email addresses out of people, and you need these email addresses because it expands your reach. You can get the email address from the people who visit your page by guiding them to click on certain links, so you don't have to ask for email addresses directly. Recommendations: Constant Contact and aWeber.

Quiz and Poll apps

These are the kind of apps that help in preparing polls and surveys to post on your page. Quizzes and polls are an important way to gain customer feedback; the more customer feedback you have, the better you can serve your customers. You need apps for this purpose because it's really difficult to get people interested in taking a short survey or quiz. Quiz and poll apps ensure that whatever you create is viable enough to attract people easily. Recommendations: Woobox and Antavo.

Automatic Posting apps

These are the apps that can be a life-saver for anyone who does not have the time to regularly update the Facebook page of their business. Automatic Posting allows you to create a post now and then schedule when you want that post to publish. The post will appear on your page automatically at the time that you set. This is really helpful because not everyone has the time to regularly post stuff on his or her page, but if you don't post stuff, your page starts to look dead. This gives a very bad impression to any customer who visits. Scheduled posting ensures that your page seems active even when you are too busy to post anything. This can be done directly on Facebook itself, or there are apps that will do it for you. Recommendations: Buffer and Rignite.

Social Media Integration apps

Social media integration is the concept of being able to use different social media sites with the help of just one app. By using these apps, you can connect different social media sites to your Facebook page, so that whatever you post on other social media sites also appears on your Facebook page. So, if you post something on your Twitter or your Instagram, it will automatically be posted to your Facebook page with the help of Social Media Integration apps. You get a lot of benefit out of this because many users follow a couple of social media sites exclusively, these users might just get connected with you on other social media platforms if they see your Facebook posts. Recommendations: Pagemodo and Tabsite.

Contest apps

Contests apps help you to organize contests on your Facebook page to increase participation in your business and keep your audience interested. Contests can be difficult to organize and take a lot of work; you even have to check the terms and conditions that Facebook has laid out for organizing contests. You can deal with all of this with the help of Contest apps because they make it easier for you to organize a contest, and they make sure that you comply with the terms and conditions of Facebook. Recommendations: Offerpop and Votigo.

Facebook Marketing

Facebook is one of the most innovative markets to use to sell your products. If you correctly tap into the platform's potential, then you will definitely be able to successfully market your products. Facebook Marketing is based on trying to capture the imagination of your audience in new and interesting ways. If you can get your audience to relate to your product, you'll be able to sell it to them.

If you have an established audience, you can definitely use Facebook to influence people so as to create a positive attitude toward your products. A lot of companies are using this strategy; they actually hire Social Media managers — people who are exceptional at handling social media platforms in order to create a positive image for the product and increase its reach. You can do all of this by yourself, however — all you have to do is understand how important Facebook is, set up your page correctly, and understand how advertising works.

Facebook is especially important for small businesses. These businesses do not have a lot of money to invest in expensive advertising campaigns. They can use Facebook to create a fan following for their products and generate enough awareness and revenue to get to that level where you can afford those expensive advertising campaigns.

Creating Facebook Business Groups

Being able to build up an online community is going to be one of the most important steps to make your business grow. It's going to help you get in touch with your key demographic. Building a Facebook page is great because it can help bring new customers to you. But, what about your existing customers? A Facebook group is going to be a great way for you to keep your existing customers in the loop. Not only that, but you'll also will have the ability to convert those that are, "just looking" into customers that are coming back for more every month!

How to Create a Facebook Group

You most likely have already created a Facebook group before. But, just in case you haven't, let's go through the steps on how to create one so that it doesn't seem so intimidating.

1. Enter the URL Facebook.com/groups into your search bar. This is going to take you directly to the set-up page so that you don't have to search through pages to find what you're looking for.

2. Click on the button that says, "create group". This can be found in the top right-hand side of the page. From there you're going to be asked what your groups goal is.

Tip: It's advised that you pick the, "connect and share" button as your goal so that you're able to keep in contact with your members, and provide ongoing support so that they continue to come back for more.

3. Enter your group name. You're going to need to name your group, and while you do that, make sure that you're naming it something that your customers will remember and mentions the name of your business.

4. Invite members to your group! Invite existing customers to your group because they will interact

with you, and because you know that they have an interest in your business.

Tip: Try to avoid adding potential customers until you've completely set the group up!

5. Set up the privacy settings. Make sure that you're not putting your group in a setting that you don't want it to be in. Open groups will be open to the public, which means that everyone can see what is posted in the group and who is in the group. Closed groups can be found by anyone on Facebook but the only people who can see what is posted will be members. Secret groups are just that, secret! The only people who can view the group's content or members will be those that have been invited to it.

6. Enter your group's description. Those that already follow your business know what your company is, but why are you creating a Facebook group? Make sure that you put a description that will tell your members exactly what to expect from the group. You'll also need to choose a cover photo for your group, make sure that your cover picture is reflecting your business properly. It's a good idea to create an image that is going to make the group appear inviting while also featuring your brand.

7. Promote your group so that others can join.

g. One way that you can promote your group is to advertise it in your newsletters and correspondence that you have with your members already.

h. Post it on your business page that you just created, and pin it to the top of the page so others can always see it.

i. If you have the budget, use boosts in order to promote your posts about the group.

j. Invite people who will be interested in your group.

What's Next?

So, now that you have your group up and going and you've gotten some members, what are you going to do next to ensure that your group continues to stay active, and you're able to engage your members?

1. Post regularly: You should post hot industry topics that your audience will appreciate being made aware of. Never make them feel like they can't ask you questions, because when questions are asked, this is going to guarantee engagement boosts while other users put their answers in the comments.

2. Share something other than your own content: When you share articles and updates that are not about your

business, your group is going to see you as authentic and an authoritative source of information.

3. Use Facebook Features: Take advantage of Facebook Live so that your customers can see the real you and know that it's someone that they can trust. This is also a great time to host a Q&A, or provide your group with exclusive insights.

4. Use ads in order to promote your group: Paid ads will be set so that they are suggested for those in your intended demographic. When you attract more members, you're going to have a better chance to widen your fan base.

Using the Facebook Business Manager

You've set up your Facebook page and your business group so, what are you going to do now? Now you should look into using Facebook's Business Manager. Facebook business manager gives you the following opportunities:

1. Work with a social agency or social media manager that will help by monitoring the quality of what is being done and keep tabs on the work that is being done for you.

2. You'll have the opportunity to have multiple accounts for your business in one place.

3. You can delegate roles and tasks to your team members so that they get done, and not everything is on you.

However, that is not the only thing that you have the ability to do with Facebook's Business Manager. This tool is 100% free and very secure, and keeps you in charge by allowing you to delegate tasks without having to share your personal Facebook with your business page.

In the end, Facebook business manager is going to make managing your business more professional.

Why You Should Use Facebook Business Manager

So, the first thing that is probably going through your head is why should you be using Facebook's Business Manager when you feel that you're delegating tasks and managing your business just fine on your own.

First, Facebook's Business Manager is going to help you gain access to your pages and different ad accounts so that different roles can be established, and tasks can be assigned to those that are working inside of your business. Even if you're a small business right now, you never know when your business will boom causing you to need help, which adds to why you should allow your team members to be able to access your business page to do the tasks that you send to them. Do not fret, as a business owner, you'll still have full control over giving permission and revoking access to people.

On top of this, it's going to allow you to keep your business pages from mixing with your personal pages so that it's a lot less awkward, and you're not accidentally posting something to your page that shouldn't be there.

Let's not forget to mention again, Facebook's Business Manager is free!

Setting Up An Account

Just as setting up your business and page were, setting up an account with the Facebook's Business Manager is easy too! Let's walk through this process together so you can get through it simply and fast.

1. Ensure that you'll be able to confirm your identity with your personal Facebook page. You need to make sure to have at least one business page as well as have an ad account that can be transferred over to business manager.

From there you're going to be able to sign up for Business Manager. Enter business.facebook.com into your search bar and once the page pops up, click on create account. Here you'll need to enter all the details for your business so that everything can be transferred over from your Facebook to your business manager.

Note: It's highly recommended to have a minimum of 2 admins for your business manager account so that the page isn't placed on just one person. This is also going to keep people from locking others out of the page in the event that a conflict arises.

2. Connect your ad account. You'll now need to connect your ad account using the following steps.

k. Click on the ad accounts on the left-hand side of your screen.

l. Choose the button that says claim an ad account in the event that you already have one.

m. However, if you're new to ad accounts you need to create one by choosing the third option on your drop-down menu.

3. Next you'll delegate the roles to employees and assign tasks throughout the account. The page admin is of course going to be at the top of the food chain and is going to be the only one who can assign tasks. From there, the managers will be able to complete the tasks that you give them, but they are not going to have full access to your page.

To be able to add a new manager you'll click settings and then pick the button that says people on the left sidebar before you move on to adding a new person.

Note: You're going to have the ability to add new managers through their business emails, but they will still be required to verify their account through a personal email.

4. Delegate tasks! Now that your managers have been added, you'll be ready to start delegating page tasks. Here's how you can do that.

n. Select pages or ad accounts. The button that you click is going to depend on what kind of task you're assigning.

o. Choose the page or account that you're granting the manager access to.

p. Next, click on, "add people" and select the managers who will be granted access to have the option of completing tasks

Next you'll have the option to assign tasks such as posting, moderating comments, managing ads, and whatever else you need to be done.

Congratulations, you have set up your Facebook Business Manager account! Once you have gone through these four simple steps, you're now ready to master Facebook Business Manager. If you still find that you need help, Facebook Business Manager offers a FAQ that will troubleshoot all of the common issues you may be facing.

Less Stress But More Control

Thanks to this tool, you're no longer going to need to worry about handling every aspect of your business because you'll have the option of handing it over to people who you trust, know what they are doing; or you may hand it over to hired social media help.

Now you'll have more time, which allows you to focus on other facets of your business so you can grow it bigger! You're a business owner, you deserve to be thinking of the bigger picture rather than being bogged down by the daily details that will lead up to that bigger picture.

Chapter 8 Instagram

Instagram is a terrific platform for building your brand. This is especially true for certain ecommerce niches like fashion and lifestyle, but not so much for others, which is why we will keep the discussion on Instagram short. Service-based brands cannot always be portrayed as effectively as products on Instagram. On the other hand, if you're building an e-commerce-based brand, then this chapter will be vital to your social media marketing efforts to showcase your brand and wow hundreds of thousands of people.

Instagram is a visual platform, so the stories and content that you will be preparing for Instagram have to be highly image-based by nature. Instagram is chock full of online shoppers who are looking for a more streamlined newsfeed based on images rather than Facebook; this is a fact that most e-commerce businesses utilize to their full advantage. Instagram also boasts a higher audience engagement rate than Facebook, which is another big plus for social media marketing in 2019. Combining the engagement rates with the fact that most of Instagram's audience is actively looking to buy something, successful marketing campaigns on the platform can and will lead to substantially higher conversion rates in sales numbers for your brand than Facebook. The only problem is that, while Facebook's algorithm can be somewhat predictable, Instagram's is a lot like

Google — unpredictable and ever-changing based on factors that move up and down with each algorithm update.

Strategies for Instagram Marketing

To run successful social media marketing campaigns on Instagram, here are a few things that you should keep in mind:

Update New Posts

Frequently update with new posts so your brand presence doesn't get pushed back by others. This means constantly creating new image-based content for your brand's newsfeed. Like Google and Facebook, Instagram also employs machine learning and AI to streamline your audience's newsfeed, so make sure your posts share relevant themes to appear constantly.

Use Images and Videos

Videos are also an important part of Instagram now, especially stories. The video duration for Instagram stories are very short, so it's best that you create a storyboard to make a structured narrative for your stories. If you have a minimum following of 10,000 people on Instagram, don't forget to add links to your stories. When Instagram stories were first launched, only big brands could add links to story posts, but now any brand entity with the above-mentioned following can add website links to stories, increasing the chance of driving traffic to your website for sales conversions.

Create Viable Marketing Strategies

Introduce viable marketing strategies that will encourage your Instagram followers to tag you in their stories. This will ensure that you constantly stay on their newsfeed, as well. On the flip side, you should also publish user-generated content that is relevant to the theme of your brand to gain bigger outreach. Unlike Facebook and Webmaster outreach methods, which require good communication skills to make the other party agree to share your posts and content, this happens naturally. Additionally, your audience feels special, making this a great technique for an increased audience outreach that is gained organically (without any paid promotion).

Use Social Influencers

Don't underestimate the power of influencers on Instagram, as they are the segment of the Instagram population that keeps the social media marketing ball rolling. To run successful social media marketing campaigns on Instagram, you need to have the best and most followed influencers within your reach. Now, there's one catch to this — hiring influencers to promote your brand can be very expensive, so you'd better have a fat wad of cash in order to hire one. Alternatively, you can provide them with free products from your brand in exchange for showcasing them, which is a tactic that works well with influencers who have a small or medium audience reach. Bigger brands often offer perks like paid vacations and photo-shoots, which can also bring down payments made to influencers. When choosing influencers, pick the ones who showcase their daily lifestyle while promoting brands, since they come off as more genuine, in turn, making the audience feel that the brand represents their regular lifestyle. Different types of influencers are suited for different kinds of promotions. An influencer specializing in luxury brands will not be effective for your marketing campaign if you're promoting non-luxury products that can be termed as average.

Show Your Instagram

Since SEO for Instagram is a bad idea in general, one thing you can do is show your brand's Instagram profile on a search engine by using Google's schema.org markup. Not only should you do this for Instagram, but you should use it for all other social media profiles of your brand on other platforms, as well, such as Facebook, Twitter, and LinkedIn.

Provide a Rich Bio

Providing a rich bio for your Instagram profile is crucial for audience outreach. Include the core keywords you have chosen for your search engine rankings in the same way you would for meta-descriptions. The bio is the only HTML-rendered element on Instagram that can be crawled by search engine bots, so this is the only valid SEO optimization you can do for your Instagram profile. Also, don't forget to add a link to the main website on your Instagram profile, though it comes with a no-follow tag by default — something is better than nothing, right? You should also add email addresses, as this has started to become standard practice when setting up Instagram profiles.

Focus On Your Profile Design

Focus on your profile design when setting up your account. Unlike Facebook, where you can have different types of content to keep the audience engaged, Instagram is all about looking good. If your profile doesn't look good, then don't expect high levels of audience engagement in your marketing efforts. Your image content should have a consistent design and editing style that will make it stand out from other brands.

Use Instagram Stories

If you can afford it, cover your brand's launch via carousels and Instagram stories. Carousels allow you to place multiple pictures one after another to form a structured narrative without appearing spammy.

Use Instagram Live-Stream

Similar to Facebook's live-video streaming option, Instagram also added a similar attribute last year as one of its platform features, though it has mostly gone unnoticed by many small- and medium-scale brands. If you're confident that you can create an attractive Live-Stream event, go ahead and do so — you will be capitalizing on something most businesses aren't. While you're at it, you can also invite influencers to take part in your live broadcasts. Some ideas for using the video live stream feature of Instagram include product launches, expert roundups, and exclusive short-term promotional campaigns that only dedicated audiences can capitalize on.

Create A Mini Video Channel

Do you wish to create your own mini video channel on Instagram, without using YouTube or Vimeo as the server platform? If so, you should consider using Instagram's IGTV feature. This was also introduced to Instagram last year, and unlike the video live streaming feature, it has generated a lot of buzz among the brands that are on Instagram, both big and small. IGTV can host videos ranging from ten minutes to an hour, depending on whether your brand profile is verified.

Dos and Don'ts

Here are some important dos and don'ts to keep in mind when putting your social media branding efforts into Instagram:

- Don't try to optimize Instagram posts for SEO. It is extremely difficult to index and rank, and even if you manage to accomplish this extremely difficult task, that SEO effort will vanish with the next Instagram algorithm change. Instead, keep an eye on Instagram insights and modify your posts accordingly to increase your outreach.

- Try to maintain an even flow when sharing posts on Instagram. If your followers are constantly flooded with your posts on their feed, it will boomerang back on you and possibly lead them to unsubscribe from your Instagram page.

- Buying followers might be a tempting way to gain access to some of the more premium features of Instagram, but don't do it. What will happen is that, like many failed business pages on Facebook, you will end up having a lot of followers with little to no engagement, which will raise red flags to potential real followers who could have been successfully converted into a sales opportunity.

- Avoid posting adult content on your Instagram posts or stories, as this will likely turn off a lot of potential followers and lead to drops in engagement ratios.

- Stick to regular marketing and promotional campaigns, but don't be too pushy. If you come off as trying too hard or create a needy image, your followers will start to doubt your brand and the quality of the products you're offering.

Don't go crazy with your hashtags. Sure, they're your primary means of connecting with audiences and letting your audience engage others with your posts, but excessive use of hashtags often backfires by distracting the audience from your intended core hashtag. This means you should drop irrelevant, trendy hashtags and instead, try using descriptive hashtags that bring out the core theme of the post you intend to share.

Instagram Basic Features

The characteristics of Instagram as a social platform whose contents are in relation to visuals. Its premises on sharing and viewing graphics, videos, and photos. Its operations and plugins are categorized on its contents: visuals. The idea that it is used only by young people is very wrong. In this section, you will be guided systematically into the features of Instagram for either beginners or professionals. By beginners, it means people that are new to Instagram while professionals mean those familiar or even have an account on the platform. Some of the basic features with their operations include:

The filter options

While uploading pictures on Instagram, the filter is the section which enables you to add enhancements on the photos to be uploaded. These filters make the pictures to look like studio edited ones. They are galvanized with features such as vintage, contrast, light, grayscale, soft glow, and lots more. Try uploading pictures and use this filter to create a special effect on them. Many influencers of Instagram claim that using these filters can make you outstanding among users of Instagram because the sense of filtration is typical only to you. Try it and grow your profile.

Like Button

One of the commonest features on Instagram is the like button. This platform can barely operate without features such as this.

This is like an authorization given to fellow users to comment, follow or do anything to your post on the platform. The like button enables users to give either pleasing or unpleasing undertone remark on your posts. With the like button, lots of transformation like increment in the number of followers and the benefits that follow is activated. The like button works in two places: it can be used on the home page, and it can be used as a user's dashboard. When the like button is used at the general page, it only gives remarks on the posts while when it is on the user's dashboard, the person becomes a 'follower.'

The Iconosquare feature

This is a form of a hashtag that is typically used to track campaigns. The performance report of the campaigns is what Iconosquare brings to you. You will be able to see relating data of the hashtag and even the growth alongside engagement of it on the campaign you have created.

The @ feature on Instagram

This is used basically for direct comment. This is for comment on posts on the platform. One could comment by tapping on the comment bubble through the person's username or type @ alongside the username.

The Word Suggestion content

This feature has been designed to help while typing on the platform. With a few words, you will be given any suggestion to make it easier for you to type. In the cases of comment, you will see related words while searching for a username. You will have related usernames.

Instagram set up operations

To download the Instagram app, one needs to consider the iOS of the medium to download it. If you have Android, you will download from 'Google Play.' If you have an iPhone, you will download from the 'App store.' Search these stores, you will, with ease, locate the app.

Registering your Instagram Account

After downloading the Instagram app, you will need to open an account. The app should create a 'shortcut icon' on your homepage after installation: if it didn't check your installed apps. Register your account or log in if you have an account already.

Creating your Instagram Account

Upon the location and clicking on the app, you will need to create a username and password. Your username can be any name combination. At this point your creativity is needed, the username can be a nickname. Care must be taken to use a name familiar to the people in order to facilitate the location and gaining of followers quickly. For example, you might consider using a clip of your first name and surname in uppercase or lowercase as 'TIMSAM' or 'timsam' for Timothy Samuel. After the username, use a password that is familiar with other platforms. You will surely need to add your email account which you could create one for the account. You can choose to add your phone number or not.

Uploading your profile photo

After you have created your account, as part of the process of perfect and strong Instagram account, you will need to add your profile picture. The picture can be taken immediately as you open your account but uploading an existing picture with high quality is highly recommended. Select 'Done' when you have uploaded the picture.

Friends and Family found on Instagram

For capitalization of your account to the full fledge, you will need to follow people that will share your pictures, and you do same to theirs. You can consider giving them your username or search from your account. With increment in followers, there are lots of benefits attached to it.

Adding and Following on Instagram

To be added to an account, you will be on the followers' list. You can follow and be followed respectively. Addition of a user will as well enable you to follow too. However, to randomly add people, you could click on the 'cog icon' on the home screen and click on 'invite friends.' With this, contacts of people around your vicinity will be suggested.

Connect to Social Media

You have an option on the app to search your phonebook directly. Simply click on 'My Contact,' and you will be prompted to search. Contacts with the Instagram account will come up, click on 'Follow' to add them to your account. Then, click on the home icon to return to the home of your account which should show the added accounts.

Home Screen

The icon looks like a house. It will automatically refresh itself when your photo has like, comment or when one of your friends add photos. The home will be updated with data, however.

Profile

The brief story created about you is your profile. The file card at the corner of the home screen contains your profile. Other things at this corner are photos, "following" and "Followers."

Privacy on Instagram

On the 'Edit my Profile' button, you can restrict the people that can view your profile. This is not encouraging, however, for a business person.

Privacy Off/on

When your privacy is turned off, anybody, even outside Instagram, can view your account. When it is switched on, only people following you can view your account.

News Feed

Photos, graphics, and videos are what is contained in the news feed. You can refresh the page by simply swiping it down. The news feeds are selected randomly; you scroll up or down.

Viewing comments from your Friends and family

The photo at the top left of your home screen is used to view people that have commented on your photo. Before clicking on it, there is something in grey color. It is meant to give you information about the comment.

Adding comment

Simply tap the speech bubble at the home screen which will prompt a new page to enable you to write your comment. Send it, and your name will appear right under the comment.

Attached Links

This feature enables people to be prompted to either another user's account or website. It is strategically attached to the account to enhance it. Most likely, it is a business account. If you click on surf new page, you can return to your home by tapping the back button on your phone.

The # Hashtag meaning

This feature is used to publicize a given post. By publicizing it, very many users will have access to the post. When you are using the hashtag, make sure there is no space between it and your post to avoid misunderstanding of your post. Additionally, when a hashtag is added to a post, it appears in blue. There are various reasons Instagram users use the hashtag. Some of these reasons include; promotion of business, gaining more followers, connecting to people that have the same idea and specialization as theirs, etc.

The hashtag enables you to search based on your specific interest on the platform. Your interest varies alongside many other things such as a book, mountain, etc. For instance, you could search with this #mountains. This will give you varying posts relating to your interest. Also, you will see profiles that have the same interest as you. The profiles that will be prompted will be top leading users who will teach you how best to construct your account too.

iOS, Android or Window icon

This particular icon is used to add photos. You can access it by clicking on the blue icon and then the circle at the bottom of the icon. Your gallery will be accessed automatically, and you can add your photo.

Followers icon

This is used to show the people that are following you in numbers. By followers, it simply means those people that your posts, whatsoever, will appear in their news feed. When you click on this icon, you will be able to see pictures of these people and either white color (to show you are following them) or blue button (to show you are yet to follow them).

Star symbols

This is technically referred to as the explore icon. It enables you to access a new page with a square at its top to type your information. With this icon, you can individualize your search. By individualizing, it means that you can search an account by hashtag or nickname. This facilitates a random and quick response from these people when you post. You can as well access their profiles upon searching.

Chapter 9 Twitter Marketing

Twitter is an incredibly powerful tool for influencer marketing, as well as many other marketing techniques. If you are already on Twitter, effectively branding your profile and learning how to leverage influencers on the platform is a wonderful way for you to begin growing into your next level of business. In this chapter, you are going to explore how you can leverage Twitter to grow your business, increase your audience, and reach the next phase of growth for you and your brand. If you are not already on Twitter, using this chapter can help you get started so that you can tap into this tool and grow your business on another great platform.

Branding Your Twitter Profile

Branding your Twitter profile effectively is an important way to make sure that you are creating a profile that is actually going to attract your target audience. When it comes to developing your Twitter reach, a well-developed profile is more clean and complete looking, meaning that people will stop and look at it longer, potentially even following you and engaging with your content. When you are developing your profile, it is important to create with your audience in mind so that they can get a feel for who you are and what you are creating. On Twitter, one study showed that more than 80 percent of people who land on your profile also check out your link, which means that this is a huge conversion you can be tapping into if you leverage your profile effectively.

There are six ways that you can brand your Twitter profile effectively so that your audience gets a complete experience when landing on your profile. These five branding tools are advanced, so whether you are new or mature on the platform, reading through these tips will help you leverage your platform and grow it even stronger.

Fill Out Your Entire Profile

With your brand in mind, make sure that you fill out your entire Twitter profile in a way that clearly reflects your brand. You can do this by ensuring that your username is on brand, your bio is filled out, and you have filled in your website information on your profile. You can also update your profile image with a properly sized branded image, header image, and background image. These three elements allow you to create a graphical aesthetic that is on-brand, making your account even more personalized and enjoyable. You should also place your city or town information in your profile so that people know where your business is located, even if you are a remote business so that you can give people an idea of where you are. Knowing where you are located helps people feel more confident that you are a real person with a location, and that you are not a scammer located overseas trying to get money from people. Essentially, it adds another layer to your online personality.

As you fill everything out, make sure that it all ties together and creates an appealing aesthetic so that your profile is visually enjoyable to spend time on. You want your profile to look attractive so that when people land on it, they are instantly curious to learn more because now you have created visual interest. You can even increase your visual interest by creating custom branding graphics for your page and switching them out every season, ensuring that your page keeps a fresh and attractive feel. Some brands will even adjust their header image every month or every other month as their specials change so that their header behaves like a promotional tool for their brand.

Follow the Right People

On Twitter, following the right people is an imperative tool in helping you generate engagement and get your name out there. When you follow the right people, you develop a group of people that you can engage with, so they begin to see who you are. As they do, they will start to follow you, giving you a following that is going to help you get started as these are the people who will start interacting with your posts as you begin posting them. Early on, really investing in the back and forth engagement process is important to help develop traction with your page, so make sure that you are spending a lot of time following people and then engaging with the people that you are following. As you do, be authentic with your sharing to ensure that you are not coming across as fake or like you are simply trying to use this engagement to grow. Even though that is part of the reason, there should also be the intention that you genuinely want to connect with these people and grow your platform.

Another way that you can use following people as a tool is through recognizing that by following the people in your industry, you are actually turning your feed into market research. When you are following all of the right people, such as people whom you look up to and people who are a part of your target audience, you get to see how your industry is growing and what is trending in your industry. This way, you can begin using the information to develop your content and keep yourself trending in your industry.

Tweet

Before you begin tweeting, there is one very important rule that needs to be made clear: *Twitter is not your electronic billboard.* Your goal when you get on Twitter is not to start blasting your wall with information and assuming that everyone is going to see what you have shared and begin interacting with you. No, Twitter is less about status updates and more about fostering interaction and engagement with your audience. You need to ensure that every update you make is not promoting your company, as this is going to come across as self-serving and spammy. Instead, make every fourth tweet promotional, and all of the others in between about engaging with your audience and starting conversations.

In addition to getting your ratios correct, you also want to make sure that what you are tweeting and how you are tweeting it is relevant to your audience. You want to use keywords that are relevant to your industry so that when people are searching these keywords, your tweets begin coming up. You should also be paying attention to trending keywords in your industry so that you can make use of these, thus increasing your chances of getting found on Twitter. Aside from that, make sure that you are using your personality and personal voice on Twitter so that people can tell you apart from the crowd.

Optimize for Mobile

Twitter is often used on a desktop, but it also has a widely popular mobile app, which means that you need to be thinking about your mobile users as well. In this day and age, there is nothing more frustrating than a business that breaks into the online space and refrains from developing any form of mobile optimization. It makes the business look incomplete and outdated since more and more people are switching to mobile devices as mobile browsers and applications continue to grow in popularity with each passing year.

Fortunately for you, the Twitter app is already optimized for mobile, so there is not much that you need to do to optimize your profile for the mobile app. The primary thing that you need to pay attention to is your graphics—since the graphics may appear differently on a mobile browser. Always take a look to ensure that you are not using an excessively tiny font or images with too intricate of details that are not as easily visible on mobile, as this can make it your profile frustrating to browse on mobile. Always make sure that anytime you update your images, you peek at what they look like on a mobile setting so that you are confident that what your audience is seeing is professional and easy to see.

Integrate Twitter Elsewhere

Lastly, a well-branded and well-established Twitter account should be integrated elsewhere beyond Twitter itself. Make sure to add follow buttons on your website, in your emails, and anywhere else that Twitter follow buttons can be added so that anytime someone comes across you online, they find your Twitter, too. If you run a blog, one particularly powerful integration is to use a plugin that allows you to feature relevant tweets in your blog posts so that people who are on Twitter can retweet your relevant tweets. This way, not only can they retweet you and get you in front of their audience, but they can also follow you and begin consuming even more of your content through Twitter, making it a win-win situation!

The Importance of Your Personality

When it comes to branding yourself anywhere online, making your personality clearly visible to the outside world is imperative. There is nothing worse than coming across a well-designed and well-positioned brand only to find that it lacks any true originality, making it sound just like every other brand that is attempting to grow in the online space. Getting your personality into your message and being authentic is an important part of really getting your message out there and growing as a personal brand.

This message applies not only for Twitter but for all personal branding strategies: if you are too afraid to speak up and be yourself, you are going to have a hard time getting heard by anyone who cares. The internet is filled with people who are afraid to be original because they are afraid to be rejected or disliked by the people around them. It can be scary to think about what might happen if you put yourself out there in a personal way and later find that you are not well received, on many levels. Even so, getting past this fear and putting yourself out there as far as your branding is concerned is necessary if you are going to get heard and develop yourself as a personal brand. You need to be willing to share your originality and show people the authentic side of you that makes you different from the crowd.

On Twitter specifically, do not be afraid to tweet with humor and share your real thoughts in relation to everything going on in the world. Talk about what you think, share your real opinions, and do not be afraid to be the real you. The more you share your authentic personality, the more people who are looking for someone just like you are going to find you and start paying attention to what you are saying. As a result, you will find yourself feeling a lot more received by your audience because they can actually find you.

As you continue sharing in this more authentic way, you will also begin to discover what types of conversations your audience enjoys having so that you know what to talk to them about. This way, you can start plenty of rich conversations through your posts, which goes a long way in terms of developing relationships with your audience. As people continue responding and developing these relationships with you, they will also continue to pay more attention to your sales posts, and will likely be more interested in paying attention to what it is that you are selling. Now, rather than just being another person promoting to them on Twitter, you are a genuine personality who is offering them a product or a service that they are interested in. You have taken the time to get to know them and develop a relationship with them, so now they trust when you say you have something that they may be interested in because they trust that you know them enough to know whether or not they actually would be.

As you can see, truly taking the time to invest in relationships online, especially on a social platform like Twitter, which thrives on conversation, you are doing your business and growth a massive favor. You want to continue emphasizing these conversations and relationships, and trust that through them, your business will grow massively and effectively.

Maximizing Growth

Once you get on Twitter, you must begin focusing on how you can maximize your growth quickly. The sooner you can develop a healthy following, the sooner you are going to be able to convert through Twitter as you will have a large enough audience to market to. Growing on Twitter is similar to growing on other platforms, although there are some strategies you can take into consideration to help you get your name out there more consistently, thus making it easier for people to find you. The thing that you need to remember about Twitter is that you need to make a big "splash" actually to get seen and followed by people. People follow those on Twitter who know how to be the life of the party, who can spark a conversation or jump in on a conversation and make it livelier, and who possess a high amount of charisma. If you want to excel on Twitter, you need to be prepared to become a loud expression of yourself so that you can be heard amongst the sea of other people who are also participating in conversations on Twitter. This is how you can go from being present to being present *and known*.

Because of how Twitter works—having a limited number of characters to use for updates and conversations—, you need to be ready to be upfront about what you are sharing from the get-go. In other words, do not waste your time burying the lead as this will result in you having your audience ignore you since they cannot get to the bottom of what you are trying to say. Be blunt, to the point, and very clear in what you are saying in every single post so that people always know what you are saying and what you mean.

Another thing you need to consider when it comes to growing on Twitter is that people are only going to see so many of the recent tweets on their pages—they are not on the platform all day every day scrolling to see what you and everyone else is saying. As a result, you can benefit from reiterating the same tweet in a few different ways to ensure that your entire audience sees what you have posted and gets the value out of the tweet that you have shared.

Make sure that you think before you tweet, as well. When it comes to thinking before you tweet, doing so can prevent you from sharing anything that may come across as derogatory or rude. For example, a company known as DiGiorno's pizza used a hashtag known for raising awareness around domestic violence to promote their pizza deals that week. They later had to issue a professional apology statement, as this came across as demeaning and rude to the people who were actually using the hashtag to promote something positive. Not all press is good press, especially in a generation of people who are becoming more and more consciously aware of how language and behaviors affect the people around them. Thinking critically about how your tweet will be received before making it is also especially important for smaller brands or personal brands who may not have as large of a following as existing corporations. For you, every follower counts, so you need to be mindful and respectful of your followers when you are generating posts.

Lastly, always give credit where credit is due as it does not come across as authentic or genuine to share someone else's content and appear as though you are attempting to pass it off as your own. Tagging the original content creator, using the acronym "RT" which stands for "retweet" or using the words "via" before sharing who originally shared the content can all help you give credit to the original content creator. Online, everyone is trying to make a living or get their name out there, so you have to be sure that you are being respectful to the other people who are also trying to generate success online. Furthermore, nothing will tank your success faster than making it appear as though you are attempting to take ownership of someone else's work. If you get caught plagiarizing content, you *will* be penalized for it, and likely very harshly. A great example of this is Audrey Kitching, who has a massive online following, and an equally massive number of people resisting her because they have found that she regularly steals content. Whether or not she actually does is unimportant; the fact is that she has become well known for this behavior and, as a result, has stunted her growth in a big way. If you stay authentic and always give credit where credit is due, then you can keep your reputation clean and your audience happy. Integrity is key.

Finding Influencers on Twitter

Twitter is another great platform for discovering influencers on, and leveraging influencers on Twitter is an equally excellent way to get your brand out there even further. Finding influencers on Twitter is similar to finding them elsewhere—you begin searching for content that is relevant to your industry, and then you start searching for the individuals who are making the biggest impact on Twitter through their posts. The key here is to know what you are looking for so that as you vet your Twitter influencers, you can be confident that you are getting the best ones. Unlike on Instagram or Facebook, vetting Twitter influencers is done in a slightly different way.

When you are looking for an influencer on Twitter, start by getting clear on the type of influencer that you are looking for. Ideally, you should be writing down what it is that they share, how they connect with your target audience, and what their personality is like. You want to find influencers who are sharing content that is relevant to what you offer, who connect with your target audience in a way that makes them likely to make sales, and who has a personality that will be a positive reflection for your brand. Finding the right influencer who is going to compliment your brand effectively is important to ensure that any money you invest into this influencer deal is going to be well spent, and you are going to get positive gains out of it.

Once you have identified who it is that you are looking for, you can begin finding influencers in your field who match these characteristics. Make sure that you are looking for people who fit these three categories first, as these need to be your priorities in whom you are searching for. You can pay attention to follower count and engagement content after—when you have identified a few people who already fit your needs as a brand.

When you are ready to begin looking at the influencer's metrics, you want to pay attention to engagement ratio more than anything else. On Twitter, a large following does not necessarily equal a large impact, so you need to be careful to ensure that the person you intend to work with does actually receive a high engagement ratio. The better their engagement ratio, the higher your chances of getting conversions through that influencer. Of course, this does come with a certain condition. If you have found someone who has incredible engagement ratios yet they are only getting engagement from tens of people or maybe a few hundred people, you are likely looking at someone who is not going to be able to create the impact that you need or desire. You want someone who has a high engagement ratio that earns them several hundred or even several thousand engagements per post, to ensure that they are someone who will make an impact. Once you have secured that fact, you can begin making content with your potential influencers so that you can start making deals with them. At this point, everything you do is going to be the same as you would have done on any other social media platform. You will still want to conduct yourself professionally, create legal documents outlining your deals, and be cooperative so that the influencer enjoys working with you and is likely to boost your reputation rather than minimize it due to your own misrepresentation of your brand.

Chapter 10 YouTube Marketing

To start working with YouTube, you have to use several steps to help you get on the site and to produce videos. Fortunately, you can get everything ready easily.

Create a Profile

Get your own profile on YouTube ready at the start. To use You Tube you need to log into Google Plus. This is the system that Google uses to give access to various online services and to be listed on Google. It is typically a good idea for a business to register with Google and Google Plus just to add your contact information and other details, but also to use YouTube for marketing.

To get your profile set, do the following:

1. Register for a Google Plus profile.

You will have to go to the Google website and click on the Sign in button to create an account. Enter a user name, a password, and your current email address and other details. You will have to verify your account with a text to a mobile number. Then you can get onto YouTube to create your own channel.

The best thing to do is to get a brand account ready. A brand account is like a personal Google Plus profile but for businesses instead. You should upload your videos through your brand account so people can see what you have to offer. Refer to the

Google Plus section of this book to see how to get a brand account set up.

As you get on YouTube, open the My Channel link on the left-hand side of the screen.

2. Click on the option to use a business or other name for your channel.

3. Enter the brand account name you wish to use.

Click on the About page.

4. Click the proper edit button on the page to enter details on what your site offers.

Be direct when telling people about the products and services you offer. Imitate the following points:

- Add keywords onto your page. This makes it easier to spot your work when a search is conducted. Make sure the keywords relate to what you are promoting.

- Explain who will post on the site and how often you might add things onto the page.

- Insert a few additional links. You can add links to other social media sites or your personal website.

7. Add a personal profile photo. Click on the small box on the top-left part of the screen to add an avatar photo. This is where people will see when you post things onto other pages.

Depending on what you entered into Google Plus, you might already have a profile photo listed. You can always change the photo if desired.

8. Add a header for your channel. Go to the top-right corner to open an option for changing the image you will display on that header. This is entered next to the avatar photo.

Go to the gear icon near the top-right part of the screen where the subscribe button is. Click and then choose to customize the layout of your channel.

Your channel page can be laid out in any way you want. Choose to add specific videos that you want to show first on a page. Additionally, sort between the view subscribers will see and what non-subscribers will notice. This lets you promote your work to others in a better light.

Get the Proper Equipment For Your Video

You could technically use a camera on a Smartphone or tablet to produce videos promoting your business on YouTube. That does not mean working with something rudimentary is a good option. The problem with such a small camera is that it will not pick up audio well. It won't produce a great picture either. You should use something a little more professional for the best results.

To get a video recorded:

1. Get a proper camera that can record well. A small high-definition camera is useful.

GoPro cameras are especially popular. Such cameras are becoming increasingly more affordable. Make sure that you know how to operate it.

Pay attention to the microphone feature on the camera. A camera needs to have a good microphone although a separate attachment might be needed if you have a smaller unit. Try to keep the microphone off-screen.

2. Look at the lighting you are using. Review how everything photographs so you can get a proper layout that looks great.

3. Look at the benefits of a video editing tool. Use it to produce a variety of special effects or overlays on your video.

You can employ various video editing programs for your YouTube video. Pinnacle Studio, Virtual Dub, and iMovie are among the top options. You could still edit features on your video directly through YouTube although it might be easier to take advantage of something more professional.

Uploading the Video

The process for recording and editing your video is clearly up to you. Next, pay attention to how you your video will be added onto YouTube.

To upload a video onto YouTube:

1. Click the download icon on the top-right part of the screen.

Select a video from your hard drive.

2. Enter the title and description.

The title should include a listing of what your video is about. It could include a keyword relating to the video's content.

The description is where you will add the detailed information on the video. It is also where you can place your business URL and other links.

4. Enter a series of tags.

The tags describe what is in the video. They can appear when someone is searching for your video. Use as many tags as you have to, but try to be specific. Refer to what you talk about in the video and location.

Click the social media links or other features that you use to share the video.

You can share your video on other sites by clicking the proper icons on the right-hand side of the upload screen. Share it on

Facebook, Twitter, or other sites connected to your profile. You can also add a message through the platform to let people know to watch your video. (Don't forget that people who watch your video can use the YouTube player to forward a video to another social media site too.)

6. Select the thumbnail you want to use.

You can always choose a random slide from your video as a thumbnail that people will see before watching your video. You can also have your own custom thumbnail that you can upload.

7. Click on the Advanced Settings section to make some adjustments.

Enter many things on the Advanced Setting section to improve how your video works. Your video can allow the following features:

- The ability to post comments.

- The option to only display comments you approve.

- Allow users to leave ratings for your video.

- Distribution settings including the option to embed a video or to publish on a subscriber's page.

- Enable age restriction; this means that you will keep underage viewers from watching your videos although you cannot promote the video in an ad campaign.

- Select the category for your video; these include entertainment, how-to, and news categories.

8. Click the Publish button at the top-right corner of the screen to get the video uploaded. It should be fully accessible to all.

Editing Your Video Through YouTube

Although a video editor can help you before you upload your video to YouTube, there might be times when you have to edit a video after it is online. This is due to YouTube's system possibly affecting the general quality of the video. Maybe you might even find an issue that you want to resolve, but you never noticed it until after you uploaded your video. Fortunately, YouTube does have its own feature to edit videos. Use this feature if you need extra help to make the video more attractive.

To edit your videos:

1. Go to the Creator Studio on your YouTube channel.

Click on the Edit button on the specific video that you want to edit.

Click the small arrow next to the button to choose what you want to edit. This takes you directly to one of the features.

3. Use the Info and Settings tab to edit the description, tags, and other features.

4. Use the Enhancements section to add light, contrast, etc.

Click on the Trim button on the Enhancements section to cut any parts of a video if necessary. This might work if you want to eliminate excess material that might not be professional or attractive.

You can do many other special things within the Edit menu under the Creator Studio section.

Adding Music

You can add background music to your YouTube video. This is great if you need some music in the background. It works better than having a plain video with silence in the background. Here's how to add music:

1. Go to the Music panel on the Edit menu of the Creator Studio.
2. Search for a track to use. You can choose something based on what is popular or on a certain genre.
3. Click any of the music files to find what you feel comfortable with.
4. Select the confirm button on the menu when finished.

YouTube has tens of thousands of music files you can use for the background of your video. These are all ad-free options to use without having to pay anything extra.

You can always use your own music to add onto your video before you upload it. That would require the use of a professional program. You would have to be aware of how the music is made and who owns the rights as you don't want to violate any copyright terms on YouTube.

Fortunately, the music files that YouTube does offer are diverse and come in many forms. They are certified by YouTube to be free for use. You will not run into any legal problems featuring these music files.

Adding an End Screen

The next thing to decide on is an end screen. This feature of YouTube appears during the final few seconds of a video. It lets you highlight other videos you want to direct people toward. Use this to get people to see other videos relating to something your business offers. Only choose appropriate videos that are relevant to the original one. This is so people see something related to their interests. Your content also has to be compelling enough for someone to click one of the videos you are promoting.

You can insert many things onto your end screen. You can add some thumbnails that link up to other videos on your YouTube channel, a link to a website, or a call-to-action to get people to subscribe to your channel.

To prepare the right end screen features:

1. Go to the End Screen section of the Video Creator Studio editor on the video of your choosing.
2. Your video must be at least 25 seconds in length to be able to add an end screen.
3. Go to the proper section of the video where you want to add an end screen.

   You can only add the end screen during the final 20 seconds of your video.
4. Click the Add Element option.
5. Select the specific item you want to add.

You can add a link to a website provided you have one that has been properly approved. You could also add a link to promote subscriptions to your channel or a link to another video or playlist.

Drag the individual items that you have added as desired.

You can move them around various parts of the screen. But watch what is on your video at the end, so you don't add these things in the wrong spots.

The end screen is great for marketing as it draws in more subscribers and lets people know that you have more to share. Use this if you have a lot of videos you want to show or you simply want to obtain some extra subscribers. Whatever your goal, you will find it easy for you to get people to your spot when the end screen is created properly.

Can You Add Annotations?

There is an Annotations listing on the Creator Studio menu, but it is not something you can use. Annotations were offered by YouTube, but they are no longer included as they cannot be read on mobile devices. Many people on YouTube preferred to disable annotations on their videos.

These features were boxes that could be added onto a video. These boxes included additional bits of information relating to something being posted. Anyone could use an annotation to add notes about what is on the screen. Fortunately, a person can easily use the end screen feature to give the same messages.

Do not be surprised if you notice annotations on older videos when comparing what your competitors might be using. Existing annotations on videos that were created before YouTube did away with them will still appear. However, they can no longer be edited.

If anything, the end screen is more convenient. It is not intrusive and distraction- free. It also offers better space for things to say and actual links that might be more valuable.

Add Cards

Adding cards allows you to ask people to send feedback about your videos among other things. A card is something that appears at any point in a video and invites people to interact. Here are some steps for producing such a card:

1. Go to the Creator Studio and then to the Card section on the space you want to edit.

2. Select Add Card from one of various cards.

   You can add a poll, a card promoting your channel, a donation card for nonprofit fundraising, or a link card that goes to your website. Any of these can work if the content you have is valuable and useful.

3. Enter the details. These include a link you want people to visit, a donation button, or a poll. The screen will produce a proper interface for any of these.

4. Choose where you want to place the card. You will have a bit of freedom as to where the card can go.

Getting your videos on YouTube up and running is easy to do when the right plans are made. YouTube has laid out everything you need right through its website. You can use all the resources YouTube provides to help you make the most in marketing your business. Best of all, much of what is offered is free to use. All you need now is a camera to record your videos. You could use editing tools on your own as well, but that's another story.

Chapter 11 Flickr

Photo sharing has transformed into an incredibly noticeable approach to manage showcase things and organizations on the web.

Flickr is one of the channels that made an impact on cutting edge exhibiting and its acclaim spread like crazy flame. It is an online photo sharing task that empowers you to incorporate your things in an interfacing way and even offers the most profitable results for your business when fused to your web based life the board structure.

Using Flickr for Digital Marketing

There's nothing more required than a few minutes to set up your record on Flickr and join distinctive people by exchanging and sharing your photos. Flickr's free record allows up to 100MB exchange each month and there is a probability for you to refresh if the free accumulating it gives isn't sufficient to you.

To empower you to take in progressively about Flickr, here is a smart look on the preferences that it can bring especially for the people who promote their things and organizations on the web.

The Benefits of Having a Flickr Account:

Huge Storage:

Flickr offers 100MB of free storing each month with the exception of you can climb to a PRO record if 100MB isn't adequate to work your necessities. With Flickr, you can exchange pictures for a similar number of as you need!

Versatility:

Flickr is a photo sharing site that engages you to make the best of your innovativeness. Next to empowering you to exchange photos, it has features that license changing of photo names, titles, and even generation of photo sets.

Never-ending Back-up:

Flickr offers the protection that you requirement for your significant photos since it surrenders an interminable back to ensure that photos will be available and guaranteed to serve your necessities.

Visitor Friendly:

Flickr isn't just for record holders since it consolidates features that empower visitors to comment on photos, incorporate notes, and watch photo slideshows. Visitors can even purchase in to RSS channel so they can see the latest pictures that you exchanged.

Extraordinary Functionality:

Flickr has a component that grants resaving and resizing of pictures. It is similarly simple to utilize so making your photos perceivable is a direct technique.

Blogging Compatibility:

Flickr also extends its degree to bloggers. Blogging is a champion among the most supported ways to deal with offer news and information. By using Flickr it will be less requesting to bestow pictures to your blog disciples.

Openness of untouchable Tools:

Flickr can be utilized using untouchable mechanical assemblies. By using free online life the administrators programming like Postific, you can without quite a bit of a stretch work with your photographs and make the best of your progressed exhibiting exertion.

Consider Upgrading to Flickr Pro

Like other web-based life accounts, Flickr offers the option for record customers to climb to an ace record that offers increasingly important favorable circumstances. Expecting almost no exertion, account holders will have the ability to get Flickr Pro and value these extra favorable circumstances:

Unlimited Storage:

Flickr Pro allows usage of limitless extra space, and that infers you can exchange photos that can outperform up to 1TB.

Photo Statistics:

By refreshing your record to Flickr Pro, you will have the ability to checks and referrer bits of knowledge for your photos. This is one of the features that a huge amount of specialists regard since it exhibits where a photo has been used or associated over the general web.

Photo Replacement:

With a Flickr Pro record, customers can replace photos without having to reupload them. They can even archive high-objectives exceptional pictures and welcome a commercial free difficulty while using their records.

Higher Upload Limit:

Flickr Pro not just offers vast limit and exchange speed, since record holders can in like manner misuse new exchange limits. Using a Flickr Pro record, photo exchanges should be conceivable with up to 200MB in size and 1GB per video.

Flickr is a champion among the most settled players and can end up a standout amongst your most dependable web-based systems administration displaying devices. Not in any way like other photo sharing goals, Flickr offers photo sharing social events. It has been used for photo sharing for a long time starting at now and remains to be the favored choice of real picture takers.

In case you are into cutting edge advancing and characteristics the power of pictures, Flickr is a decision that you can't stand to reject. Use it with an electronic life the board gadget for business and undoubtedly, you will have the ability to develop brand care no problem!

Chapter 12 Tumblr

Tumblr is a fabulous stage to achieve a large number of potential clients. When choosing whether Tumblr is directly for your web-based life advertising efforts, you generally need to figure, by what method will it advantage your clients. In this part, I will breakdown what Tumblr is, and how you can utilize it further bolstering your good fortune.

What Type of Platform is Tumblr?

Tumblr is a cross breed blog arrange and casual association. Customers can post media content (photos, delineations, chronicles, music, GIFS, etc.) to a blog, seek after each other and comment on each other's posts. (You do have the decision to make your blog private.)

Who Utilizes It?

Customer numbers are hard to tie, yet work it to express that numerous people use Tumblr – which stunned me! Dependent upon the source, Tumblr has 300 million or barely short of 500 million web diaries, web journals and 400 million or 600 multi month to month customers.

Most customers are around the world – only 65% of development begins from the US. Customers are in like manner energetic – youths and Millennials. So it ought not stun anybody that a bigger piece of customers visit the site from their phones. Thus, in case you are attempting to contact people some place in the scope of 13 and 30 years old far and wide, genuinely, use Tumblr.

How Does Tumblr contrast from Facebook and different stages

The gigantic focus on Tumblr is quality over sum. Building critical associations and teaming up with various customers is unquestionably more fundamental than having a zillion aficionados or fans. So in the event that you will use it for advancing, you should concentrate on successfully enamoring with different people.

In like manner realize that it's stacked up with claim to fame systems and subcultures, immense quantities of whom have their own one of a kind eccentric lingo.

The most effective method to utilize Tumblr for Marketing Your Business

Pick a Catchy Name

Tumblr web diaries will when all is said in done have smart, sly or critical names, as Tor VPN Bear. Everything considered, there's nothing out of order with using your picture name. Additionally, it'll help with brand affirmation.

Get Creative

All around advancing messages on Tumblr won't go over well. You ought to be inconspicuous. Discharge your creative side and post content that is useful, hopeful and happy.

Continuously Provide Links to Your Site

For sure, it is OK to offer associates with your site, especially in the event that you're running an unprecedented progression. Basically, ensure those presents are more close on home than what you may continue running on Facebook or Instagram.

Try to Pay Attention to Customers Wants and Needs

The better you know your social event of individuals, the better your substance will do on Tumblr – just like some other stage. What questions do your social event of individuals have? What information do they strive after? That is what you need to post on Tumblr.

Utilize Tags

Marks and labels are comparably as basic on Tumblr as hashtags are on Instagram – they'll empower your substance to get found in interest. 10 to 15 labels for each post is flawless, just guarantee they're look terms that people are using.

Become dynamic

Since quality collaboration is so basic, the more you put in, the more you'll get out. Seek after various locales and leave comments. This will raise your detectable quality and help you pull in supporters.

Chapter 13 Goodreads

Goodreads is an incredible informal community where millions interface by means of their writer page, yet it isn't just for writers, we can utilize this site for web based life promoting purposes too.

How has Goodreads turned out to be so broad? All things considered, similar to Amazon, individuals can locate their preferred books and see fair audits. It resembles an extraordinary enormous virtual Facebook, Barnes and Noble store with Amazon folded into one.

When you open a peruser account on Goodreads, you fundamentally can tell different adherents what books you like, what books you are right now perusing and even make gatherings and subjects identified with your preferences, post surveys and the sky is the limit from there!

To get to know Goodreads you should simply agree to accept a record at www.goodreads.com and after that start investigating. The site will walk you through the methods for utilizing it, Goodreads is very easy to use. There is no cost to joining, and is a huge amount of fun!

So have you joined? Stunning. Here are some ways you can Goodreads for advancing your business.

1. Setup an Author Page

Time: 1-2 hours

Getting an essayist page is the underlying advance to connect with your perusers on Goodreads. Consider this your Facebook page anyway on Goodreads. Making an author page will give you experiences about your books and will give your perusers a spot to see what you are up to and what you are scrutinizing.

You can find how to join the Goodreads Author program. This page has point by point headings that will walk you very much arranged through the setup strategy.

2. Solicitation that Your Readers List Your Books on Listopia

Time: 30 minutes

The Listopia portion of Goodreads has a summary for each kind of book conceivable. Guarantee your books are on the best possible records.

You can find this portion at:

http://www.goodreads.com/list

Every now and again the differentiation some place in the scope of 30th and tenth on these once-overs is only two or three votes. So the more your perusers vote the higher your books will rank.

3. Advance

Time: 1 hour + $20

This is optional anyway worth the effort. Goodreads has a pivotal book-advancing system that empowers you to target people who have very assessed unequivocal scholars. Are your books like

James Scott Bell? You can concentrate on his fans with an ad for your book.

You can in like manner use this instrument to target people who have assessed your books previously. You may have fans who loved your diverse books and who have no idea about your latest book. Goodreads empowers you to connect with those perusers.

The advancements can cost as small as $0.15 per click. This is a standout amongst the most affordable ways to deal with enlighten your perusers concerning your new book.

4. Do Book Giveaways

Time: 1 hour + books + shipping

All things considered; 850 people enter each Goodreads book giveaway. Of the people who enter, they will add the book to their to-examine rundown and half of the victors will complete a survey for the book. Goodreads has a book giveaways region arranged unequivocally to empower you to expose issues about your books.

5. Setup Groups and Discuss Books

Time: 1 Hour

Goodreads empowers you to have a book exchange about your book. This empowers your perusers to make request and talk with each other about your book. This is an unprecedented technique to change lukewarm perusers into eager book evangelists. You can be as connected with these book trades as you should be. The key is to start the discourse and after that let your perusers take it starting there. For the methods on the most capable strategy to start a book trade, visit Goodread's Featured Books.

6. Interface Your Blog to Goodreads

Time: 20 minutes

Did you understand that Goodreads will email your fans once per multi day stretch of all your new blog sections? This is a phenomenal strategy to help perusers for you blog for all intents and purposes zero work. Basically, set it up once and subsequently you don't need to worry over it. Blog blend is one of the preferences you get when you join the Goodreads Author Program.

7. Approach fans for legit Reviews

Time: 30 minutes

GoodReads features books reliant on the amount of studies. Try not to fear negative audits. The most basic thing these days is the amount of reviews. The more audits your book has the more popular it looks. The more noticeable it looks the more people read it.

Begin utilizing Goodreads today! This site is best stayed quiet diamond in web based life promoting

Chapter 14 The Best Way to Approach Social Media Marketing

Sometimes, even when you follow all the necessary steps, you may not get as many online engagements as you desire. So, here are a few tips and tricks to drive online traffic.

Use hashtags

Hashtags are basically tag to help find things of a similar nature in one place. This is precisely why you should always use hashtags with your promotion, since it will help your post reach beyond your network to people searching for similar items or services. This is especially useful when using Twitter or Instagram to promote your brand.

Email marketing

Email marketing is often one of the most overlooked methods of driving online traffic, but this should not be the case, especially since technology has allowed over 3.8 billion people to use email. Moreover, people now use email apps that have their own custom notification sounds, making it quite impossible to avoid noticing when emails are received.

Analytics

Free-to-use analytics like Google Analytics are a great way to increase online traffic. If used properly and regularly, these can accurately show you which strategies and types of content work the best, in turn, giving you an idea of what to improve and what to let go of.

Backlinks

Backlinks are links to your website or products from another website. These are great to use to drive online traffic. Backlinks enable your website to be exposed to a bigger audience than your own network. Moreover, trust from Google increases on your backlink with the more trusted websites that point to it, leading to a higher ranking and more exposure and traffic.

Google search advertising

Although this is a paid option, it can be a great one to use for driving traffic to your website. The way this works is that you will have to pay Google a certain amount of money for your website to be included in the top search results for certain keywords.

Stay updated

The best way to drive traffic is to stay updated with what is happening in the social media world. You should always find out which hot topic everyone is talking about, and then you can use this information to your advantage by tying your products or services to that topic. Not only does this drive more traffic, it also creates a positive image of your brand in the minds of people who view your posts.

Conclusion

The world of Social Media is a constantly evolving one. Competition is good though because it brings about disruptive innovation. That's why each social media platform is constantly enhancing and introducing new features to stay relevant to its audiences, giving them better tools to share their content, better ways to engage, and more interesting ways to publish content.

One of the best ways to engage in social media marketing for your business is first to use it as a personal platform for personal use. Use it as an experiment, play around with it, upload images, and get used to it before you embark on opening up an account for your business. This way, you'll be better equipped to make a decision whether that particular social media is worth your time and effort or not and you will also know how audiences in different platforms react to content.

Social Media Marketing, on the other hand, has many benefits, and it does a lot to improve site traffic and help a business reach more customers. Not only that, social media marketing helps brands have a better understanding of their audience and learning from them- their purchasing habits, their likes, dislikes, interests, and so on.

Any business stands a chance to lose out on its customer base if they do not evolve with current times. That said no business would lose out by investing in social media.

www.ingramcontent.com/pod-product-compliance
Lightning Source LLC
Chambersburg PA
CBHW070316240526
45467CB00045B/285